A Dolphin of Many Colors
An inter-species friendship

By
Jennifer Semro

Published by Dolphin Defenders
Bonita Springs, Fl.

Published by:
Dolphin Defenders
PO Box 933
Bonita Springs, Florida
34133

First printing 1996

Cover by: Robert Perkins

Library of Congress Catalog Card Number 95-92553

ISBN 0-9648672-0-6

**A look at captivity
viewed throught the
eyes of the dolphin**

Acknowledgments

Brenda Peterson:
Author of "Living by Water" for the first encouragement to write this book.

Robert Perkins:
For the first of many words of encouragement and support, and a wonderful cover.

Doreen Clark:
For recreating the cover design that was lost with Roberts death.

Russ Rector:
Former dolphin trainer and head of Dolphin Freedom Freedom Foundation, for his generosity of time and information about captive dolphins.

Sandra Yeyati:
My editor, who took an outline and helped me transform it into a book.

Stan Nippert:
For final preparation of text and graphics.

Alison Anderson:
My close friend who listened, and encouraged when I needed it most.

The following people have all contributed to this book in one way or another. I have listed them in alphabetical order, not in order of importance.
Ken Balcomb, Mark Berman, Angelo Cane, Kim Carson, Alex Diaz, Leon Eisenbud, Toni Frohoff, Arthur Hale, Tom Hayer, Meg Hutchins, Vicky Impellemone, Jeff McCann, Gordon McMullen, Lana Miller -*Author of Call of the Dolphins*, Jane Piasecki, June Riggs, Mark Roberge, Jan Sherlin, Rick Spill and to my family and friends who have supported this effort.

Contents

Chapter

Dedication

To the memory of Robert Perkins who designed the cover. Regrettably he did not live long enough to see his work published. He passed away in February of 1996.

He was a wonderful friend.

My children in the order of their appearance:
Kelly
Mark
Julie
Richard Jr.
Toni

My grandchildren up to the present time:
Ashley Pink
Ian
Olivia
Phoebe
Eric
Alexandra
Nicholas
Corinne

And to the dolphins of the world that inspired me to write about them.

This book is presented to

_____

From

_____

Date _____

**The true essence of LOVE
is freedom
and the desire
that the ones we love
be happy;**

Alpha
Greek Origin

First or Beginnings

Alpha

Sometime in the future: In a small village in Greece

"There are no survivors, there are no survivors." He could hear the words pounding in his ears. After all this time and it still felt as if swords were piercing Peter's heart. The air felt chilly as he walked along the beach with his memories, but the warmth of the sun surrounded him like a blanket. The sand appeared to have crushed diamonds that reflected the sun, and felt so good on Peter's bare feet. He watched the birds feeding on the shells that were brought in by the gentle waves of the sea. Peter tried to concentrate on tomorrow, his twenty first birthday, and the gift his friend Orpheus promised to give him - a boat of his very own.

Orpheus had been a friend of the family for

as long as Peter could remember. He treated Peter like the son he never had. Orpheus was a quiet, private person who had never married. He lived in a modest home in a secluded part of the village. The surrounding trees hid not only his home, but a small section of beach, that allowed him the privacy he cherished.

Peter's thoughts drifted back to the day, five years ago, when Orpheus became more than just a friend. His parents planned to fly to a small, neighboring island for a weekend getaway. They did not like the idea of Peter staying by himself even though, at sixteen, he was very mature. Orpheus agreed to stay with Peter until their return. That Sunday Peter spent the day on the beach, watching the birds, and daydreaming on the warm sand. He promised Orpheus he would be home before dark. Peter's pace quickened as he approached his home and saw Orpheus standing in the doorway. He was hungry, and Orpheus had promised to prepare dinner. Peter watched Orpheus slowly walk toward him, he knew by the look on Orpheus' face that something was terribly wrong.

Peter could feel his heart pounding as he cautiously asked, "What has happened?"

Orpheus put his hands on Peter's shoulders. "Son, there has been a terrible accident. Your parents were on their way home, something went wrong with their plane and it crashed into the sea. A search team has been looking all day, Peter. There are no survivors. I am so sorry."

Peter looked at him in disbelief. His face distorted with the pain he felt, "No! This can't be true." He began to sob.

Orpheus took Peter in his arms, and they both wept. He then pulled away, with tears still on his cheeks and said, "Peter, I have always loved you as a son. I know that I can't replace your parents but I want to help in any way that I can. Please come and stay with me."

For a time, Peter did live with Orpheus, but eventually he found a place of his own. The two nevertheless saw or talked to each other almost every day. Orpheus continued his role of surrogate father, for which Peter was most grateful.

Sometimes he sat and gazed out over the water. His thoughts were of his parents and how much he truly missed them.

Peter and Orpheus spent the past year restoring an abandoned vessel they found by Orpheus' home. Peter remembered the first time he saw the boat laying on its side, in the sand. It was a dingy gray, with vast amounts of sand and salt residue. Seaweed clung to the bottom in varied patterns. Peter inspected the craft for exterior damage while Orpheus examined the interior.

"I wonder who it belongs to," Peter said.

"It looks as if it has been here for some time," replied Orpheus.

"Could we keep it? We could fix it. I didn't see any major damage on the outside." Peter looked at Orpheus with anticipation.

"Well", Orpheus pondered with his hand on his chin," we could take it to my garage but if someone is looking for it we'll have to return it. We'll wait thirty days and if no one claims it, it will be ours. On second thought, if you work on it with me," Orpheus said smiling, "it will be yours on your twenty first birthday."

Peter jumped up and down with excitement."Yes, Yes, I will! I promise!"

It was far too heavy for the two of them to move, so they waited until high tide, at which time they loaded it onto Orpheus' boat trailer.

Once safely stored in Orpheus' garage, the seemingly endless thirty days passed with no inquiries about the craft. They began to prepare the boat to be sea-worthy. Orpheus rebuilt the tired engine. Peter scrubbed and polished the interior until it glistened. Together they painted the exterior teal. The many hours they spent together made the bond between them even stronger.

Tomorrow, Peter would test it on the water for

the first time. The excitement he felt would not allow for much sleep tonight. This would be the beginning of a new way of life for Peter. He planned to seek adventure on the water, and learn about the mystical life that existed in the sea. He could hardly wait. The next day as Peter approached Orpheus' home to claim his treasure, he saw his friend standing beside the boat with an expression of sadness, as if he were saying good-bye to an old friend. Peter thought that today Orpheus looked older than his fifty years. His stature was more muscular in contrast to Peter's long and lean frame. He had thick black hair and a handsome beard that he kept neatly trimmed. His eyes were deep blue and filled with wisdom. At one time he had smoked a pipe but now settled for just keeping it in his mouth as a pacifier.

Orpheus smiled as he saw the young man approach, "Happy birthday Peter," he said.

Their eyes met, in mutual understanding of what this day meant. For Peter it was a freedom he had dreamed of for most of his young life. For Orpheus it brought a twinge of sadness. He would miss the many hours they had spent together this past year working on the boat. It had turned out even better than either of them had expected. Twenty feet long, with a two hundred horse power engine, so clean that it sparkled in the sun, and the exterior the color of the sea. At last it was ready! Peter was glad that Orpheus' home was at the water's edge, where he could temporarily keep the vessel.

Peter walked around the boat scrutinizing every inch, the way a mother checks her newborn for the correct amount of fingers and toes. He noticed a beautiful silver dolphin painted on the bow. The word "Stenella" was printed under it.

"What does stenella mean?" Peter asked.

"The word comes from the Greek word stenos, which means narrow. There are several species of dolphins that have long, narrow beaks that are referred to as Stenella. Most of them live in the deepest waters."

"Oh."

Orpheus looked at Peter and smiled. He had shared many stories with Peter about how, years ago, bottlenose dolphins could be seen from shore. But now their numbers had dwindled and sightings were rare. In his lifetime, Peter had never seen a dolphin.

Both he and Orpheus struggled to push the trailer to the water's edge. They gently guided the Stenella into the water. The moment had arrived and Peter's heart was pounding with excitement. He turned the key, and the engine responded immediately. As he maneuvered the boat around, he took one final look inside to determine that he had everything he needed for his first adventure on the water, including the life jacket that Orpheus had insisted upon.

He waved farewell, as he slowly moved the Stenella away from shore. His thoughts now focused on all of the sea life that was directly beneath him, from the smallest crustacean to the largest whale. He wondered what it must be like to swim with no boundaries.

The water reflected the color of turquoise. As he became more comfortable guiding the Stenella, he began to go faster. The wind blowing through his hair felt wonderful. For the moment, he didn't have a care in the world.

The clouds formed various patterns. Some looked three dimensional. They appeared to be suspended in the sky by invisible threads. The billowy white puffs were surrounded by beautiful blue sky. Some looked like streaks of white smoke that were propelled by drifting winds.

He wished that Orpheus had come with him, but despite Peter's many requests, Orpheus refused. He felt sad and did not understand why on this most important day his closest friend insisted that Peter go out on his own. He felt in his heart that something was not right, but he didn't have any idea what it could be. Had he said or done something wrong?

After he was several miles offshore, Peter changed course. The Stenella now traveled parallel to the shoreline. He did not want to venture too far out on his first journey. The color of the water changed to a dark blue which indicated that it was deep.

Out of the corner of his eye, he thought he saw something very large pass under his boat. It rapidly crossed back and forth at the bow of the Stenella. He tried to watch it but it swam as fast as his boat.

He waited to see if it would reappear. Peter wondered what it was. Could it be a shark? His eyes desperately searched the water. Then he heard a whooshing sound. He looked in the direction where he thought the sound came from but he still couldn't get a clear view. He slowed the Stenella but the creature also reduced it's speed, again swimming back and forth across the bow.

Peter shut off the engine and looked over the side. At first he couldn't see anything, then suddenly, it came directly towards his craft. Peter was frightened. What was this creature and what was it about to do? It swam directly underneath his boat again, but this time it came to the surface. He heard the strange whooshing sound once more. Without warning the creature leaped completely out of the water.

Peter was amazed at what he saw. It was huge. At least eight feet long, It's body a beautiful deep blue-gray. He saw a fin that projected from the middle of its back. The animal's underside was white with a hint of pink, with additional fins protruding from each side. It reentered the sea with barely a splash.

Just as quickly as the creature appeared, it was gone. Peter tried to contain his excitement, but he was almost sure he had just seen a dolphin. Peter started the engine and sped to shore. He was eager to share his news with Orpheus.

"Peter, are you sure what you saw was a dolphin? They are social animals that live in families and rarely travel alone."

"At first I thought it was a shark, but when he came to the surface to breathe, I knew it wasn't."

"It might have been a bottlenose dolphin. They grow to be the size you describe, and usually stay close to shore."

A few days later Peter took the Stenella out again, eager to find the dolphin. This time he ventured out farther. Today there was not a cloud in the sky. Seagulls flew overhead, acting as escorts.

Peter noticed one bird in particular that was smaller than the rest. He would plunge towards the water looking for food and then glide along the surface. Each time he failed to catch a fish he vocalized his frustration. This behavior led Peter to believe he must be a young bird. Finally the immature gull's persistence met with success. A small anchovy from a school of hundreds could not escape even the clumsiest of his attempts

The little gull was not the only one looking for breakfast. Directly underneath him was a gray form, following the same school of fish. Because the water was crystal clear Peter could see that this looked like the dolphin he had seen a few days before. He watched as the mammal propelled his body forward with an up and down sweeping motion of his fluke, unlike the fish all around him whose tails moved from side to side. Peter was amazed by the dolphin's grace and how quickly he could change direction. As he watched, he realized that this was not a stenella. Although its beak was prominent, it wasn't long or narrow as Orpheus had described.

The dolphin appeared to study the fish intently, and then swam through the school snatching the ones he wanted. Peter saw the many cone shaped teeth as he threw a fish high out of the water and then caught it in the air with his mouth. It appeared that he had turned eating into an exciting game.

As the school of fish, began to swim away

from the Stenella, so did the dolphin. Peter thought, "Please don't go." He wished that somehow he could communicate his thoughts. He closed his eyes and visualized himself diving into the water in pursuit of the dolphin. The water felt cool and refreshing as it passed over his body. His legs together formed the shape of the dolphin with his feet acting as the fluke. He thrust his legs in the same sweeping motion. He felt his body being propelled forward. He was closing the gap "Please wait," he thought. The dolphin turned and hesitated. Peter came closer. He was within arm's length and looked into the mammals soft brown eye. "Please come back, I want to be your friend!" Appearing to understand, the dolphin allowed Peter to gently hold onto his dorsal fin, and they slowly swam toward the Stenella.

Peter opened his eyes. Expecting to see the dolphin, he leaned over the side of the boat looking for any signs of his presence. He listened for the sound the mammal made when he surfaced for a breath. His eyes scanned the sea around him. Nothing.

Disappointed, Peter decided to guide the Stenella home. He began to pull the anchor aboard but it seemed to be caught on something. He leaned over, balancing his body on the rail, to get a better look. Suddenly a huge form came up and out of the water within inches of his face. He fell back on the boat with a thud in time to see his beautiful new friend thrust his body high out of the water. The dolphin landed on his side as he reentered the sea with a splash. Filled with joy, Peter exclaimed, "You came back!"

The dolphin swam alongside the Stenella and raised his head from the water, looking directly into Peter's eyes. Peter felt a great emotional rush as if a warm wave were passing over him.
He knew that this was the beginning of a unique relationship. He decided to call his new friend Alpha, because it was the first dolphin he had ever seen.

On his return, Peter asked Orpheus to share everything he knew about dolphins.

Motioning to the tall stack of books in the corner of Orpheus cluttered bedroom, he said, "You are welcome to take the ones you want."

"I have never seen these before."

A long time ago, I too was in love with the sea and all of its' creatures. I especially loved the dolphins.

Peter thought he detected pain in Orpheus' eyes as he spoke. "They became a big part of my life. Someday I will tell you all about it."

During his studies, Peter discovered that dolphins belonged to a group of animals called Cetacea, derived from the Greek word cetus,

meaning whale. Peter was surprised to learn that
the dorsal fin he had held in his fantasy contained
no bones, was very sensitive, and was used for
balance. The pectoral fins that had altered the
course of the dolphin toward the Stenella,
contained a bone structure similar to the arm,
wrist, and hand of a human. They were also used
to vent body heat and to caress each other.

He learned that Alpha tossed the fish in the air
for an important reason. Despite numerous teeth
he did not chew his food. The fish had to be
swallowed head first or the fins and tail would cut
his throat.

Peter and Orpheus spent many hours talking
about dolphins, although Orpheus would not
discuss his relationship with them. Orpheus
exhibited a strange sadness whenever he talked
about them.

"Dolphins have guided boats to safety,
rescued swimmers from drowning, even rescued
animals. Many people don't realize how
intelligent dolphins are. A dolphin's brain is
slightly larger than a human's."

Two weeks passed before Peter took the
Stenella out again. He guided the vessel over the
waves to the place where he believed his friend
Alpha would be. He circled the area several times
before he spotted the familiar fin. This time there

was not just one, but many fins surfacing above, and disappearing below the water in synchronicity. He rubbed his eyes in disbelief. He counted one, two, then six, seven, ten, eleven, fifteen in all. Alpha had brought his whole pod to meet Peter. Tears welled up in Peter's eyes. He realized that this beautiful animal trusted him to do his family no harm.

Peter was so caught up in the excitement that at first he did not notice Alpha swimming differently today. Then he saw that something was attached to Alpha's dorsal fin. As Alpha swam closer Peter identified it as a piece of fishing net. Although it was small, some seaweed had attached to it and was acting as a weight. He realized his friend was in danger. The net would continue to collect debris. The only thing for him to do was to get in the water and try to remove it. Would the dolphin allow him close enough to help? He had to try.

As soon as he entered the water they all turned and swam away. The water was cold and, unlike the dolphins, Peter did not have a thick layer of blubber to retain his body heat. It was several minutes before they returned, cautiously keeping a safe distance between Peter and themselves.

He took a deep breath and submerged. He felt a strange tingling sensation, and heard whistles and clicking sounds. This must be the echolocation that he had learned was so important to their lives. One of Orpheus' books had described how the sound was projected from the melon of the dolphin, until it reached an object. Information such as size and location reflected back, was received through the lower jaw, and sent to the brain. Peter thought it must be like having a camera that developed the picture instantly. He wondered what the dolphins saw when they used echolocation on him.

Every time Peter came to the surface to breathe, he tried to focus on making Alpha understand that he wanted to help. The dolphins cloistered around Alpha forming a protective circle. When Peter tried to approach they moved just enough to maintain a safe distance. He thought about the day they met and tried to project images that would make Alpha understand. Peter was cold and tired; he had trouble focusing. He knew that he couldn't remain in the water much longer. He pulled himself on board, shivering, and wrapped himself in a blanket. He turned the Stenella toward shore and thought, "I will try again tomorrow."

The next day the waves were higher when Peter looked for Alpha, which made it difficult to spot the fins. Finally the dolphins appeared. Peter had worried all night about Alpha. As he scanned the group looking for his friend he determined that Alpha was not with them. The dolphins were swimming erratically. They all swam off in one direction and then returned. They swam off again, then they stopped. Peter started the engine and slowly moved toward them. They waited and when he got close, they took position as a group in front of the boat. They were enticing Peter to follow them.

They led him to a shallow bay. Now he knew why. He could see a dolphin just ahead. It was Alpha struggling to free himself from his burden. The net had accumulated floating kelp and sea grass and was caught on something. The top of Alpha's dorsal fin was sliced almost through by the twine of the net. He was held so tight that he could barely get the top of his body wet. Peter shut off the engine and dropped the anchor. He entered the shallow water and saw that the mass Alpha dragged was tangled around a line from a crab trap.

Talking softly, he slowly approached Alpha, "Don't be afraid," he said. "I won't hurt you. Let me get close to set you free."

Alpha eyed him suspiciously, but could not move. As Peter got closer he saw blisters forming on the dolphin's skin from being in the sun.

He was within arm's reach. He continued

reassuring Alpha, "I won't hurt you. Please trust me." He took his pocket knife and cut the line that held Alpha. The moment he was free, he turned and swam away. Peter felt the power from the dolphin's tail, propel him backward. Peter had cut away the mass but the net was still attached to his fin. Now that Alpha was free, "How would he get close enough to remove it? "I don't know how" Peter thought, "but I will find a way." Within minutes the dolphins returned, again keeping a safe distance from Peter. Alpha cautiously swam over and stopped directly in front of him. Peter reached out and touched the dolphin. He was amazed at how soft but firm the skin felt. Alpha hovered long enough for Peter to remove the net from his injured dorsal fin. Then he dove alongside of Peter brushing his body.

Peter threw the net onto the Stenella. With a squawk, one of the seagulls swooped down from the sky and snatched it. The bird flew overhead in circles exhibiting his trophy. Suddenly dolphins were leaping out of the water, swimming under him, next to him, jumping over him. Peter exclaimed,"It's a celebration Alpha!" They swam close, without touching him. He was glad to see them back to the business of enjoying life to the fullest.

A Dolphin of Many Colors

*   *   *

For the next several months Peter spent many happy hours and days swimming with, and getting to know Alpha's pod. They allowed him to watch the very close social structure of their lives. He saw how they interacted with each other showing love and respect. They were very physical with each other, almost always touching.

Peter began to understand how they communicated and learned from one another. They identified each other with whistles. He watched them play, tossing objects freely from one dolphin to another. When they communicated, the same behavior was exhibited. They waited their turn, without interrupting each other.

Peter felt clumsy when he swam with them. The grace that they exhibited left him in awe. He could not keep up with the pod. Sometimes they slowed to accompany him. They mimicked whatever he did. If he did a somersault in the water, so did they. If he turned his body around in a spin, they would do that also. Sometimes he stayed under water until he felt his lungs would burst. The dolphins surfaced to breathe every two or three minutes. That was beyond Peter's capacity.

What wonderful creatures they were. He felt

so privileged to be allowed in their company. Of all the dolphins in this pod, Alpha was the only one that allowed Peter to touch him. Sometimes when Peter became very tired, Alpha offered his deformed dorsal fin and the two would glide through the water.

When he was aboard the Stenella he saw how they foraged for food. First they detected a school of fish through echolocation. Then the pod separated and each dolphin took a position around their prey. The positions changed as each individual passed through the school of fish to feed. Again, they showed respect for one another during this process. What a wonderful way to live, spending most of their time eating and playing. They seemed to have no enemies.

*   *   *

It was June, almost a year since Peter and Alpha had first met. Peter had come to know Alpha's pod very well. He could identify each member by the shape of it's fin or a distinguishing mark. Peter lazily enjoyed the quiet of the water. He floated the Stenella among the playful dolphins, and reminisced about all that had happened since their first meeting. Peter spent most of his time on the water now. He felt like he was becoming a part of their lives. They certainly were a big part of his.

As he watched the dolphins, he noticed that two of the females maintained a distance away from the rest of the pod. There seemed to be much excitement going on between them. One of the dolphins was in some kind of distress. What could be happening? He decided he would try to see if he could help. He entered the water and noticed that one of the females was periodically spinning as she swam. He saw a small tail extending from her body and realized he was witnessing the birth of her calf.

Another female stayed very close to her and vocalized continually, as if to comfort her. Peter remembered reading about the female companion called auntie that played an important role, helping the new mother. Finally the newest member of Alpha's pod arrived. It's dorsal fin was still folded over from the birth process. Peter smiled at the awkwardness of the calf's swimming ability. The mother and auntie stayed on either side of the calf as it surfaced for its first breath of life.

Peter did not know whether it was a boy or girl but it seemed healthy and strong. Because it was full of energy and appeared excited to be alive, Peter named the little calf Apollo.

He saw the love and tenderness the female

exhibited toward her offspring from the moment it arrived. He called her Aphrodite because she reminded him of the Greek goddess of love. Apollo instinctively found the "baby position," between his mother's pectoral fin and tail, slightly under her body. Auntie, who would help to teach Aphrodite important mothering skills, also swam close by. From his studies Peter knew that Apollo would spend the next 18 months nursing and bonding with his mother. He would probably stay with her up to six years. He had much to learn from her, as well as his siblings and older pod members. For now he remained close to Aphrodite.

Off in the distance Peter saw other fins in the water. At first he thought it was another pod coming to participate in the jubilation. All the dolphins became excited, sending out signals to each other. As these new fins approached, Peter saw that they were different from the dolphins. They moved along the surface in a continuous line. These were not dolphins, they were a school of shark! The birth of Apollo must have alerted them.

Peter immediately climbed onto the Stenella. Fear gripped his heart at the thought of what was about to happen. Could the dolphins defend themselves against this group of predators? They were large and outnumbered Alpha's pod.

The dolphins clustered in a tight circle with the baby in the center. The males protected the outer wall of the community. The sharks swam in a larger circle around them. Peter was filled with terror, and felt so helpless. He looked frantically for something to throw at the sharks. He never filled his boat with items that he didn't absolutely need and felt sorry about that now. He picked up his life jacket and hurled it as hard as he could at the ominous group. It distracted them only momentarily.

The dolphins' squealing and the snapping of sharks' teeth was deafening. The violence that ensued in the water caused waves to hit the Stenella and sent Peter sliding to the other side. As he got up, he saw Alpha race toward the attacker closest to him. With his powerful beak he hit the fish directly in the abdomen. Although the shark was stunned, it turned so quickly that Alpha never saw the jagged teeth inflict a serious wound on his side. Peter saw blood in the water.

Was Peter witnessing the death of his friend? The rest of Alpha's family fought for their own survival. Alpha again charged with his beak, although clearly bleeding badly and losing strength. Peter saw something race through the water and thrust its body into one of the sharks, nearly tearing it in half. Was this another shark?

It looked too large to be a dolphin, and it was very light in color. Everything happened so fast. The creature charged again, this time killing the largest of the attackers.

The battle was over as fast as it had begun. Being scavengers, the rest of the sharks focused their attention on the bleeding carcass. The dolphins took this opportunity to escape. Peter followed them with the Stenella. As Peter approached Alpha's pod he saw that the creature that had killed the shark was a dolphin, the largest he had ever seen. It was as white as the foam on the crest of a wave. There was much activity in the water. Whistles, clicking and a white dolphin that seemed to reassure each of Alpha's family. Then Peter saw his friend being supported by two pod members. Aphrodite was following close behind with Apollo at her side. Alpha's injuries were severe, and Peter could see the pain in his friend's eyes. The white dolphin took charge, and Alpha's pod was led away. Peter wondered if he would ever see his friend again. His heart felt heavy as he guided the Stenella home.

Aristotle

Greek philosopher

The first man to classify the dolphin as a mammal.

Aristotle

Peter told Orpheus the details of the day. As he relayed the story, he could see that Orpheus felt his pain but remained silent. Peter described his rage when the sharks first attacked, his frustration when he was unable to assist them, and finally his sadness when he realized he might lose Alpha. Peter's description of the large white dolphin prompted Orpheus to tell the story of the only white dolphin ever seen by man.

"Many years ago an albino dolphin lived off the Atlantic coast of the United States. Because this dolphin was pure white, people called her Snow. To see her was considered to be a good omen. The fishermen and people of the town all loved her. The stories of Snow spread far and wide.

"At that same time, a new type of entertainment was becoming very popular. Mammals such as seals, whales and dolphin were taken from their natural homes and placed in marine parks which consisted of small pools with artificial habitat. The captive animals were trained to perform tricks for food, and the public paid to watch them.

"A park in the southern United States heard about Snow and thought that she would be a great attraction. They mobilized a team of the best dolphin catchers in the world to take her. They descended on the town and tried to capture the white mammal but she was very clever and outwitted them many times. The men would not give up as it meant a great deal of money for the park and prestige for them.

"The townspeople were outraged. They did not want Snow captured for any reason, and vowed to protect her.

On a cool summer day, the water glimmered like a sheet of glass. Only the gentle breeze created ripples. Snow had not been seen all morning. The boat moved through the water with almost no sound.

"Finally one of the men whispered, 'I see the white fin.' They all looked in the direction he was pointing. 'Where?, I don't see anything,' whispered another. 'I think it's your imagination,' said a third. They all strained to see something. 'There it is again!' This time two others saw her as well. 'Get the net and be ready! We don't want to lose her.'

They positioned their boat so that when they lowered the net into the water Snow would be between the net and the shore. The net was twenty feet from top to bottom and one hundred feet in length. Buoys were attached to mark the net's position. Below the water it would appear as a continuous barrier from the surface to the soft bottom. One man held the net over the side of the boat and released it gradually as they slowly cruised along, making sure that the net was completely submerged, with only the buoys visible.

"Snow was feeding, and unaware of the men's activities. She was used to boats, and didn't fear people. The men slowly dragged the net toward shore and shallow water. Snow swam along the edge of the net. She was still in water that was deep enough for her to dive and swim away. As the men brought the net closer to shore, the area for retreat was diminished. When they reached waist deep water, the men slipped over the side of the boat and surrounded her.

"One of the men took the boat to an area that was hidden by tall grass and dense trees near the water's edge. He dropped the anchor and swam back, joining in the capture. When Snow realized that there was no escape, she panicked. Her eyes darted wildly looking for a way out. She was not trained to jump over things, and echolocation told her that the net was an impenetrable wall. She tried to dive but the water was too shallow. She slapped her tail in protest.

"The men slowly approached her. One held

her just above her tail, another was at her head. Suddenly she stopped all motion. Maybe she thought that if she didn't struggle the men would set her free.

"Most of these men had captured dolphins many times, and had learned the best way to subdue them with the least amount of damage to their sensitive skin. They physically held her so she could not escape. An uninjured dolphin that survived the stress of capture would bring at least twenty thousand dollars.

"No one noticed the townspeople gathering on the bridge behind them. Something hit one of the men in the back of his head, he immediately put his hand over the area and felt something warm and wet. When he looked at his palm, it was covered with red. The air was filled with spoiled fruit and vegetables directed at Snow's would-be captors. The men quickly dropped the net and held their arms over their heads. They came out of the water as fast as they could. The townspeople waded in and pushed the net to the bottom freeing Snow. Then they gathered it together and carried it away with the promise that it would never be used again. Everyone cheered.

"Later the boat was destroyed by fire. No one was sure how the fire started, but some very familiar buoys were found in the water close by.

"Because the eyes of the community were

watching, the dolphin catchers knew it was futile to risk another attempt. Several days later, a boat picked them up, early in the morning, and they departed.

"The townspeople sought to protect Snow from future attempts to capture her. They held a meeting and passed a resolution to protect any dolphin within the city limits. It was the only place in the entire country that prohibited the capture of a wild dolphin. Violations were punishable by a large fine as well as incarceration.

"The following year there were no attempts to capture Snow, so the townspeople began to relax. As mid-summer approached, it was rumored that she had a calf. Since the incident last summer, Snow had kept her distance from humans, so no one knew if it was true. And if there was a calf, they wondered whether it too was an albino?

"One evening in late summer the police received word that boats had been sighted just outside the city limits. They looked very similar to the ones that had tried to take Snow the previous year. By dawn the next morning the boats were gone.

"Snow had not been seen for weeks and finally the sad news was announced. To everyone's dismay Snow had been lured away, and captured. If there was an infant, they didn't know whether it too was taken, or left behind. Without its mother survival was doubtful.

"Her captors were right, Snow became a great attraction. People came just to see her. Her trainers said she was the most gentle of all the dolphins. But, despite all their efforts, Snow never performed for an audience. She died 3 weeks after her capture. Between the stress of living in captivity and the loss of her family, she seemed to lose the will to live. Snow was fifteen when she died, one third of her expected life span in the wild. No one has seen an albino dolphin since.

"This is why I ask you, Peter, are you certain about what you saw today?"

Peter took a few minutes to digest all that he had just heard. He looked at Orpheus intently and said, "I have spent a year with these animals, I know them, and I am positive."

Orpheus placed his hands on Peter's shoulders and said softly, "I think you have been chosen to see this exceptional mammal for a reason."

On the walk home that evening, Peter thought about Orpheus' words. He was saddened by the events he had witnessed today. If he were chosen to do something, as Orpheus had suggested, why couldn't it have been to save his friend?

Peter slept very little that night. He was up before dawn and ready to begin the search. The morning air was cold and full of moisture. He had never been on the water to see the sunrise before. It was beautiful. As Peter watched the sun surface above the water he hoped that it signaled a rewarding search. But, it was almost dark before Peter and the Stenella returned with no sign of the dolphins.

Had the sharks scared them away? Orpheus told him that dolphins have a long and vivid memory. Maybe they would never return to the same area, associating it with such devastation. Peter decided to broaden his search tomorrow.

Peter scrutinized the sea for days with no sign of Alpha, his pod or the white dolphin. He watched large schools of fish pass the Stenella, expecting hungry dolphins to be close by. He saw jellyfish and stingray. Occasionally he observed a school of shark, methodically scanning the sea for a meal. But, no dolphins.

All week the sky had been filled with seagulls. Peter did not question why, until a single bird came to rest on the rail of the Stenella. This seagull looked like the one who had seized the net, that injured Alpha. The little bird apparently was interested in Peter and what he was doing, while the rest of the flock remained airborne. Could they also be looking for the dolphins? Each day Peter guided the Stenella to the area where he last saw Alpha and his family. Everyday, the little bird joined in the vigil.

Peter grew tired from the strain of his continuous pursuit and, as the boat gently rocked, he closed his eyes and drifted off to sleep. He awoke with a start, to the sound of thunder and realized that he had slept into the middle of a storm. The clouds were dark and the sea had changed from a calm beautiful blue, to an ominous black. He attempted to retreat to the safety of the shore. The waves pounded against the Stenella with great force. Peter had no experience with the violence of a stormy sea and struggled to keep the Stenella on course.

A bolt of lightning crashed from the sky. Peter felt it's energy throughout his body. He smelled something burning, and as he looked over his shoulder, he saw a small fire in the corner of the craft. He grabbed a bucket and filled it with sea water. He threw the water on the flames, but the fire grew. His attempts to put it out were futile. He looked up toward the dark clouds in anguish hoping it would rain. The fire grew larger, and Peter realized that within minutes he would have to abandon his beloved Stenella. He cut the engine and grabbed his swim fins, snorkel and mask. Now he wished he had the life jacket.

He heard the fire crackling as it consumed his craft. He looked out over the water and wondered how far he was from shore. From his position he could not see any land. He was an excellent swimmer, a talent which he hoped would help him survive. He remembered Orpheus telling him to always remain calm. "Panic makes people do foolish things," Orpheus had warned. Peter wondered whether throwing his life jacket at a school of shark would apply?

He put his swim fins and face mask on, took a deep breath, gathered all the strength he could and jumped off the Stenella for the last time. He swam as fast as he could to escape the intense heat from the fire, but the swells were large and made it difficult to put distance between the boat and himself. As he did, the water became cooler, and felt invigorating.

By now the wind subsided and it started to rain. He swam for some time at a steady pace. After a while the storm ended and the sun was shining once again. The sea was calm, and Peter was relieved. He guessed that he had been swimming for about two hours. He had paced himself but was very tired and didn't know how much farther he could go.

Peter began to believe that he would not survive. His legs felt like they were weighted, and he could no longer move them. As he slipped farther under the surface, the snorkel began to fill with water. Memories of his life with his parents, Orpheus and Alpha flashed through his mind. He felt like he was falling into a dream-state, a beautiful dream in which he saw Alpha, Aphrodite and Apollo. The sun streamed through the water, illuminating the trio. As he descended deeper into the water, he saw Alpha come closer, with Aphrodite at his side, followed close behind by Apollo. As he passed into an unconscious state, he had the sensation of being weightless. He was floating. Then he realized that somehow his body was being supported. Was this a dream, or some kind of hallucination that preceded his death?

He felt something soft pressing on the back of his neck and became aware of a presence on either side of his body. He could feel a vibration going through him and recognized the whistling sounds. As he turned, he saw that it was, Alpha and Aphrodite. He was overcome with joy. As he looked closer, he could see the wound on Alpha's side. It had healed but left a large ugly scar. His friend had survived and they were reunited. Apollo was tucked in next to Aphrodite's pectoral fin. It had turned out to be a wonderful day after all.

Peter enjoyed the clarity of the water and all the wonderful sights and sounds of the sea that the dolphin experienced on a daily basis. He began to realize that this day was very different for him. Not only were the sights appearing different but the sounds took on a new meaning. He realized that he was able to see and hear as the dolphin did. To communicate, they transmitted visual images among themselves. Peter was amazed that, for the first time, he understood these images.

Alpha guided Aphrodite, Apollo, and Peter through the water. Peter did not need to come to the surface for air any sooner than the dolphin did. How was this possible? Alpha swam alongside Peter and communicated to him, that the next time they surfaced, Peter needed to breathe deeply and rapidly. They were going on a very deep dive, and would need to have their lungs completely filled with air. Peter did as he was instructed. He sensed that something powerful was about to happen.

As they began the dive there was very little communication. During their descent Peter was struck by the beauty all around them. Colorful fish and plant life he had never seen before were now visible. He felt intense pressure against his body, causing his ribs to collapse. Alpha detected Peter's apprehension through his sonar abilities and reassured him with a stroke of his pectoral fin. As they continued deeper and deeper, the water was the darkest of blues, almost black.

Then, in the distance, Peter saw a stream of light through the water. This seemed impossible because they were at least 1,000 feet under the surface. As they approached, the light became more brilliant. In the center of the radiance a form became apparent. It was the largest and most exquisite mammal Peter could have ever imagined. He realized at that moment that this was the white dolphin that had saved Alpha.

He was magnificent. His skin was flawless. His eyes were pink, as was his tongue. When he opened his mouth, he revealed many black, cone shaped teeth. How odd that his teeth are so dark, Peter thought. The creature gazed at Peter with an intensity, but at the same time a gentleness. Peter was unafraid. He still wondered whether this was a dream.

Peter was filled with many questions for the dolphin. He projected several of them at the same time. "Who are you? Where did you come from? How is it that I can understand your language?"

The white mammal responded: "I will answer all your questions in due time. I was born many years ago into a small pod of coastal dolphins. When I was born my skin was a very pale gray, not at all like my parents; or the rest of my family. It was thought that in time my skin would darken like the rest of the group. Instead, it became lighter until eventually it was pure white. I was much larger than other dolphin calves, and lacked the aggression to lead groups of young males.

Although my family loved me, I knew that I was different and longed to find someone more like myself. It was decided within the pod that when I reached maturity I was free to go on my search.

In my twelfth year, I began a long and lonely pursuit to find a female like myself. I desperately missed my family but I knew that I had to continue. After searching for many years, I found her, a gentle, beautiful, creature. We swam together playing with sea kelp and feeding on schools of fish and shrimp. When we prepared to return to my home territory and my family, we discovered that she was due to give birth. We decided to stay where we were until the calf was born and weaned. Our trip was delayed about eighteen months.

"One day as she was feeding, some men came with boats and took her away. I could hear her whistles of distress in the distance, but I was afraid to get too close with the little calf. We never saw her again. Something told me this would never be a safe place for us. So, we made the long trip home with much sadness in our hearts. When we arrived, my family welcomed us, and the females in the pod took our calf and taught him well. He has now grown strong enough to go out on his own." He looked at Alpha with love and pride.

Peter realized that Alpha was the grown son of

Snow and this beautiful white dolphin! Because of his apparent wisdom Peter called him Aristotle.

Peter said, "I have heard about a white dolphin called Snow, who was loved and protected by many people. Despite their efforts, one day some men came and took her. No one knew there was more than one white dolphin. Snow did not survive. She died a short time after her capture."

"Why did the men take her away? Aristotle asked. "Where did they take her? What did they want her for?"

Peter wanted to explain, but he didn't understand it either. Peter saw Aristotle's pain and wished that there was something he could do to help.

"My son has shared the stories of the relationship that has developed between you. We are grateful that you helped him in his time of need. We wanted to repay you, when you were in danger."

"How is it possible that I can understand your language?" Peter asked.

"When my son and his companion found you in the water, they placed a special seaweed at the base of your neck, which allows your brain to receive messages at the accelerated rate of speed needed to perceive our language."

"Why do the dolphin stay so far away from shore? I understand that long ago they played close to the water's edge and allowed humans to swim in their company."

"Many species of dolphin around the world are disappearing faster than they can reproduce. You see, we can not bear young until we reach maturity which is sometime between the age of seven to twelve. It takes approximately a year before a calf is born. Most of the time the first born do not survive and the females cannot produce another offspring for at least two years. I have chosen you to be our spokesman to help save the dolphin nation."

Peter was astonished! "What can I do to help the dolphin?"

"You can educate people about us and what is happening to us. We have already started to educate you."

Peter did not know what to say.

"We need to understand the changes that are occurring in our waters. Many are uninhabitable. Many dolphins get sick and die. There are things we need to know. Maybe we can help each other." "I've been told that there are men in our waters as we speak. We do not know why they are here."

Peter was excited by Aristotle's proposal. He also felt proud that Aristotle had chosen him to help.

"Now, you must go. Be careful as you return

to your boat. You will keep the perception of the dolphin for 24 hours, then the essence of the seaweed will dissipate and people will again perceive you as human."

Peter looked at Aristotle with amazement."The Stenella was destroyed by fire."

"I assure you Peter that the Stenella is intact and waiting for your return."

Aphrodite and Apollo stayed with Aristotle, while Alpha guided Peter back to the surface.

*   *   *

They had almost reached the Stenella when Peter heard Alpha's whistle of distress. Peter had been so distracted by all the beautiful sea life around him, he had almost forgotten about Alpha. As Peter turned toward the cry for help he saw that Alpha was unable to swim.

As Peter approached Alpha he could not understand what held him captive. As he got closer, Peter looked for some kind of barrier, but none was visible. Meanwhile Alpha sent out the message: "Danger, danger!" Peter was about to touch his friend when he realized that Alpha was entangled in a net that was almost invisible, even to the dolphins' highly sensitive echolocation. As Peter tried to free Alpha, he became entangled as well. Alpha panicked. This time it was Peter who tried to reassure his friend.

Peter remembered that he would be perceived as human again in 24 hours. Peter indicated to Alpha that if they could survive until dawn, he could free them when his human form returned.

Peter let Alpha know that they needed to stay very still so as not to entangle themselves any further. The net allowed them the freedom to surface for air. Fish were also caught in the net, some had already died. Peter hoped that no sharks were in the area. This night would be one of the longest of their lives.

At dawn Peter heard the noise of an engine in the distance. The sound became louder as it approached. It frightened Alpha. He tried to dive, to escape but Peter communicated to stop or he would make the situation worse. "You must remain calm," Peter projected. The noise grew louder, then suddenly it stopped and Peter heard men talking.

One man said, "George look over here, we have two dolphins caught in the net!"

"Are they alive?" George asked.

"Yes."

"We better let the authorities know."

Peter heard all this, he became concerned about his transformation. If it came now how would he explain it?

Above, he heard his little friend, the seagull,

squawk as he soared high in the air and then dove briefly close to the water. He did this again and again. Then, just as quickly as he had appeared, he flew off. Crazy little bird, Peter thought.

More noise approaching, many motors, noise in the air too. The water became violent with motion. Countless boats and a helicopter circled the area. Fear gripped Peter's heart as he saw no escape for Alpha or himself.

During the night Alpha had begun to get sick and, the more stress he experienced the worse he got. Peter was glad to see the boats come. He hoped that they would be rescued. In the meantime, he encouraged Alpha to continue to breathe. Orpheus had explained that dolphins didn't breath automatically. Peter knew that each breath was a conscious decision.

Boats were all around. Several men jumped into the water and swam over to the netted captives.

One of the men saw Peter and said,"What a beautiful animal."

Another man said, "Look at this one, the whole top of his fin is missing. I wonder how that happened?" As he put his arms around the dolphin to hold him still, he felt Alpha's scar. "Look at this," he said, "he has a huge nasty looking scar. This guy's seen his share of trouble."

The men held Alpha so that his blow hole was

above the water, and freed him from the netting. Peter begged Alpha to hang on, assuring him that he would guide them both to safety once they were released.

Off in the distance Peter heard whistles and clicks in the water. He breathed a sigh of relief. Pod members were on the way to help them. The dolphins would come and escort Alpha home as soon as they were free.

Next the men concentrated on Peter, cutting the net carefully away from his skin. Both animals were free of their bonds but the men did not let them go. One of them yelled, "Lower the stretcher, we'll take this one first." Peter realized that it was him they were talking about!

The stretcher was a piece of canvass wrapped around two long poles, with a large opening on each side. The men lowered it into the water. As some of them held Peter tightly, others placed the device under his body. They positioned his pectoral fins through the holes. When this was done, Peter felt himself being lifted out of the water. For the first time he felt the weight of his body. Peter did not understand what was happening. He was frightened and confused.

He was surrounded by men who placed him on a hard surface. One poked his fluke with something and said, "This will calm him down until we get there." Peter could not understand why these men had not set him free. What did they want?

Alpha was placed next to him. He struggled slightly and his breathing was labored, indicating stress. He whistled, calling out to his pod members. Two men poured water over the pair, in an attempt to keep them cool.

The little seagull returned squawking and carrying on, as if to communicate something to Peter. On one of his passes he flew so close that his beak almost touched Peter. The next time he flew directly over and deposited something on Peter's neck. The man who had been keeping Peter cool was startled by the seagull's behavior. He attempted to stay out of the line of fire.

"That bird obviously has a problem," he said, "Maybe someone should do away with the pest." The gull as if he heard, quickly flew off into the clouds. The man looked at Peter and said, "That's strange, that bird just dropped some seaweed on your neck."

Now Peter understood that the bird was a messenger sent by Aristotle. From now on Peter would call him Hermes. The little gull had brought seaweed to extend his experience as a dolphin. Peter did not think that was a good idea.

*　　　*　　　*

It seemed like a long time before they reached their destination. Because of all the movement the animals were experiencing, their skin became irritated. The area under Peter's pectoral fins began to bleed.

When the boat stopped, there was much excitement. More men came to examine them and one said, touching Alpha, "There is a foul smell coming from his blowhole, we need to take care of this one first, he's very sick." Alpha was then carried away by four men.

After a while they came for Peter. He was lifted and carried in the stretcher. The ride was bumpy as the men walked with him.

He felt himself being lowered into the water, but somehow this water was different. It didn't sound like the ocean . The only thing Peter could hear were the motors that sounded similar to the ones he had heard this morning, Two women supported Alpha in the water and talked to him softly. In his state Alpha could not appreciate their compassion.

Peter saw no beauty in this water. A continuous barrier surrounded him. It was a very small space. Peter felt confined and confused. He tried to swim forward, but in a matter of seconds he needed to avert the barrier. He then tried to dive but it was too shallow. He could not understand why they would be kept in a place like this. He tried to use his echolocation, but the sound resonated back to him and caused some discomfort. No sound, no beauty, no food, no space. Why had Aristotle abandoned him and his own son, Alpha? Why didn't he let Peter resume his normal form to save himself and his friend?

Orpheus

Greek Mythology

Qualities of dynamism and creativity through water.

Orpheus

Orpheus had not heard from Peter for three days and was concerned for him. Peter was spending countless hours on the water. The sea could be dangerous for a novice captain. Orpheus decided to rent a boat from his friend at the marina and search for Peter. He remembered Peter's description of the area where the dolphins were usually found. Although it had been a long time since Orpheus navigated these waters, he thought he knew where to look.

Orpheus approached the marina, his thoughts focused on Peter. The boat was ready and waiting when he arrived. As he loaded his supplies on board, he caught sight of the name painted on the vessel. A chill ran through his body. The Seeker. "How appropriate," he thought.

Orpheus had forgotten the joy that the sea brought him, especially on a glorious day such as this. The sun had evaporated most of the morning fog, and the calm water sparkled like glass. Under different circumstances, he would have enjoyed this day. Instead he was anxious over Peter's disappearance.

The sea reminded him of things he had done in the past, of which he was not proud. What would Peter think if he knew the truth about Orpheus and his relationship with dolphins? Maybe Peter had found out about his past and had chosen to stay away. Orpheus would never forget that period of time and the consequences it brought.

As he continued out to sea the memories came flooding back. He remembered his parents, hard working farmers, always struggling to make a living. Neither of them had the time or inclination to show affection towards Orpheus. He learned at a young age to obtain the love he so desperately needed from animals, domestic and wild. Every morning when he did his chores a menagerie of creatures accompanied him. Even the birds knew Orpheus.

When he was nine years old his mother left with no explanation. Orpheus was devastated. He couldn't understand why she would leave him. Had he done something wrong? Was it his fault? For weeks he cried himself to sleep. Although they had not enjoyed a close relationship, he loved his mother. On the occasions that he asked his father for answers, his dad would get an angry look on his face and reply, "I don't know, son, I just don't know." Orpheus never saw his mother again.

Because his father could not work the land by himself, he sold the property, and they moved to a small seaside town. His father found work on a fishing boat, requiring him to be out at sea most of the time. Orpheus was miserable, in a new town and alone. It was a very difficult transition. His animal friends were sold or left behind.

He began to spend time by the water. He learned to swim, finding an inner peace when he was there. He grew to love the sea and learned about all of her creatures. He became a proficient diver. Over time he learned to control his breathing and could stay under water for as long as four minutes. He befriended sea creatures as easily as he had on the farm. He studied the reefs and their inhabitants. By the time he reached manhood, word of his accomplishments were known by many.

One day as Orpheus was walking along the beach, an unfamiliar man approached. He extended his hand and said, "My name is Joseph Bach." He had a slight build and a firm handshake. His pale skin revealed that he seldom spent time in the sun. He had a disproportionately large nose and was bald, except for a small, comical patch of hair in the center of his head.

"I have traveled a great distance to meet you," he said. "I am in charge of a large marine park, and would like to offer you a job. I understand that you have a special talent with sea animals."

Orpheus was stunned. He had a thousand questions. "What is a marine park? What kind of animals do you have? Why would you take them from their homes?"

Joseph placed his hand on Orpheus' shoulder. "Slow down son. A marine park is a place where we keep animals on display to educate and entertain people. Primarily, we keep dolphins."

"Don't they suffer in captivity?"

"No, in fact they seem quite happy. There are no predators to harass or kill them. We feed them high quality fish regularly, which is not guaranteed in the wild, and have a vet available should they get sick."

Orpheus listened intently.

"We only hire people who love animals and have a special talent like you, Orpheus."

"Where would I live?"

"We would provide you private living quarters on the park grounds. People come from all over the world to see our animals perform. I am seeking a trainer and I believe you are the best."

"I don't know anything about training animals. I observe them where they live. I have never even touched a dolphin."

"We have a group of ten dolphins at all times. My head trainer, Hans needs an assistant. He will teach you everything you need to know."

Orpheus was confused. He shrugged his shoulders and shook his head in disbelief.

"I need an answer by Monday," Joseph said. "Take the next couple of days and think about it." Orpheus spent time in the water, hoping the answer would come to him. He had mixed feelings. He loved the idea of having so much contact with the animals, and felt it was important to educate people about these magnificent creatures. He hated the fact that they were denied their freedom. In the open waters he often swam with dolphins, but they never allowed him to touch their bodies. He guessed that this park was huge, knowing that dolphins swam great distances. By Monday he had his answer. Orpheus couldn't wait to tell his father about the great opportunity he decided to accept. Orpheus expected his father to be happy for him. He was surprised to find a look of sadness as Orpheus told him about his plans.

"I hope that you have made a wise decision," his father said.

"This is what I want to do."

"I will miss having you here."

"I promise, I will write often." Orpheus worried about his father who was never the same after his mother's departure. In the past year he had grown tired and listless.

He felt an obligation to stay with his father, but this opportunity sounded too good to pass up. As he began to pack he thought about his good fortune. At twenty-three this would be the first time he would be on his own. To earn a decent income doing what he loved, it was ideal. He looked forward to living a better lifestyle than he had been used to.

His first day at the marine park was etched in Orpheus' memory. It was early morning, raining lightly, as he walked through the big gate. The first thing he noticed was the strong smell of chemicals. Directly in front of him was a large concrete pool. The bottom and sides were painted a vivid blue, creating the illusion that the water was also this color. It was circled by rows of bleachers. Off to the right was a small building. Orpheus approached the door that read "Office" and knocked. From inside he heard, "Come in." As Orpheus entered he noticed the walls were filled with pictures of dolphins. How beautiful they were. The room was neat and clean except for Joseph's desk, which was cluttered with stacks of paper.

Joseph stood up extending his hand to Orpheus and said, "We have anxiously awaited your arrival."

Orpheus smiled as he pulled his chair closer.

"We are all like family here, there are no formalities, so you can feel comfortable and relax. We will teach you all you need to know to be successful."

Orpheus nodded.

"You will need to know everything about the animals. You will be responsible for cleaning the tanks and preparing food for the dolphins. I will introduce you to Hans, our head trainer. He has been with the park from its inception and does an excellent job with the dolphins." I don't have much time today, but, we have a very important project coming up and will need your expertise. We will discuss that later.

Orpheus couldn't imagine what Joseph was talking about.

Joseph always seemed to be in a hurry.

The longer Orpheus studied the man across from him, the more he became aware of a coldness in Joseph Bach's eyes. Orpheus tried to dismiss this negative feeling about his new employer. He must have many responsibilities, taking care of so many living creatures, Orpheus thought.   Joseph rose from his seat, prompting Orpheus to do the same.

"I will show you where you will be staying."

The two men walked behind the small office to a row of cottages. When they reached the third one, Joseph opened the door to a small apartment. As Joseph was about to leave he said, "Hans will be over to meet you in a little while. He will show you what to do and help you get familiar with the park." With that, Joseph turned and left.

Orpheus closed the door of his new living area and felt very pleased with himself. He looked around at the old, comfortable furniture, sat down and closed his eyes, just for a moment.

There was a loud banging on the door. Startled, Orpheus awoke, and stumbled over to open it. As he did, a large, stern looking man leered at him.

"What were you doing? I have been knocking a long time. I am a busy man, do not keep me waiting!"

Orpheus was embarrassed. "I'm sorry, I have traveled all night and did not get much rest."

"Hmfp! Well, lets get going"!

Hans was about six feet three inches tall, and probably weighed 300 pounds. He was as gruff as he was big. Although Orpheus was six feet tall, he felt overpowered by this man. He had thick blonde hair that continually fell over his eyes.

They entered a small room that resembled a kitchen.

The smell of fish was overwhelming. One man stood over a deep sink cleaning a mackerel that looked like it weighed twenty pounds. He didn't acknowledge Hans or Orpheus.

"This is where all the food for our animals is cleaned and prepared," said Hans. "Every fish that comes in here needs to be examined. Lately we have found foreign objects still embedded, such as fish hooks, which must be removed. We also insert vitamins and medication."

"Are one of the dolphins sick?" Orpheus asked.

"No," said Hans, "and that's the way we want to keep it."

Hans walked to the far end of the room and opened the latched door of a large cooler. Buckets of fish lined the shelves. Bold letters identified to whom the food belonged. Another door at the back of the cooler exposed a sizable freezer filled with fish, some whole, others in pieces. There must have been a thousand pounds of fish in that freezer.

"Be here tomorrow at 5:00 AM. I will take the correct amount of food from the freezer and put it in the cooler to thaw for you in the morning. You will inspect it again before it is cut and rationed. All fish must be ready before the first show at 11:00 AM."

Orpheus nodded that he understood.

Hans took him to the main show pool, but no dolphins were in sight. He told Orpheus to sit on one of the benches. Hans disappeared through a gate to the left of the pool which led to another tank. Orpheus heard the squeals and clicking of dolphins. When Hans opened the gate, a huge bottlenose dolphin raced through an underwater opening into the pool. Hans climbed up the ladder to a platform positioned directly over the water. He took a bucket with him. The dolphin swam around the pool, picking up speed and creating a whirlpool. Water spilled over the sides splashing Orpheus' feet and legs. Hans took a small fish from the bucket and placed it in his mouth as he held up his right hand. The dolphin dove to the bottom of the pool, and with great momentum leaped out of the water and snatched the fish from Hans' mouth.

Orpheus could hardly believe his eyes. For the next few minutes this exquisite animal performed spins, raced around the pool, leaped through hoops and seemed to be having a wonderful time. Orpheus couldn't wait to learn how to train these animals to respond for him. What a wonderful job he had. Hans motioned with his hand and arm for the dolphin to go back through the gate. The dolphin obeyed. Hans came off the platform with a big smile.

"This is what we want," Hans declared, "Perfection!"

Hans invited Orpheus to see the other dolphins who were kept in three small pools connected by wire gates. Deteriorating paint and rust stains covered the walls. There was a single dolphin in one of the tanks, two in the adjoining pool, and five in the enclosure closest to Orpheus.

In all, he counted eight bottlenose dolphins of various

sizes, including the huge animal that had just performed. He observed that all of their dorsal fins were lopped over. He never remembered seeing that on a wild dolphin. They were kept in cramped quarters and continually swam in circles. He remembered that Joseph had said there were ten dolphins. Orpheus wondered where the other two were, but didn't ask.

"Each tank has a purpose, "Hans explained," The first one on the far end is a holding pen used primarily for new arrivals. This is where they get used to the human touch and learn to eat dead fish. Usually it takes about two weeks for them to become acclimated. Then they go into the middle tank where they learn to live in close quarters with other dolphins, and we observe them for any aggressive behaviors. The third tank is used for training. While we are training one or two of them, we allow the others to play in the main show tank."

In the far corner was a small pen that couldn't have been more than eight feet long and three feet wide. Orpheus pointed to it and asked, "What is the very small enclosure used for?"

"If one of our dolphins starts to get out of hand, we just put him in there for a few days, cut back on his rations, and ignore him."

Orpheus frowned in disapproval as he listened to how the dolphins were punished.

"That's one of the worst things that you can do to a dolphin. After a few days they'll do almost anything for us, they're so glad to see someone."

"Isn't that harmful to the animals?"

"Well, we do have to be careful how long we leave them in there. The first time we did this was with a stubborn male, who would not cooperate. We kept him in there for five days. The sixth day, when the trainer attempted to feed him, the dolphin refused to eat. He was losing weight so we had to force feed him" Orpheus felt an ache in the pit of his stomach.

"He was so stubborn that the moment the trainer turned his back, he regurgitated what had just been forced down his throat. The trainer was angry and frustrated. He reprimanded the disobedient animal. The dolphin looked at him, shuddered, and took a final breath. We think that he committed suicide. Since then the isolation tank is not used for more than three days at a time."

Orpheus felt sick inside. He was glad that this kind of treatment was in the past. He would not let any of these animals be abused while he was here. He thought that perhaps Hans was exaggerating to a degree. What could these animals ever do to justify such treatment?

Hans introduced Orpheus to Dennis and Jason, with whom he was to work until he became familiar with the routine. Both were muscular. Dennis was tall and slender. His curly dark hair accented his brown eyes and boyish smile. Jason looked younger. His eyes were small and piercing. He had a mustache that camouflaged an uneasy smile. His demeanor was stiff. Jason appeared agitated and distracted. He didn't look at Orpheus when they shook hands.

Later Hans said, "Don't mind him, he has an attitude problem."

*   *   *

Orpheus was up at the crack of dawn brimming with excitement. He met Dennis at the fish room, where he learned to inject medicated capsules into the food after it was prepared.

"Why do we give the dolphins medicine?" He asked.

"To help relieve stress. Many dolphins have a hard time in captivity. When they are stressed they are susceptible to disease."

"Oh," said Orpheus, but he still did not understand. He was confused but told himself that the experts must know what they were doing.

The fish were ready by 10:00 AM. Dennis took Orpheus to the showtank.

"Jason did not show up today, so there will be extra work for us." Dennis handed Orpheus a pair of swim fins.

"Is Jason sick?"

"I don't think so," Dennis response was vague. He slapped Orpheus on the back and smiled, handing him a scrub brush. "This is Jason's job, but today you get to do the honors." Dennis pointed to the tank, "See the algae on the bottom?"

Orpheus nodded.

"You need to remove it with the brush."

Orpheus put on the swim fins and jumped off the side of the tank with brush in hand. This was the first time he had been in the water since he left home. He was used to the sounds of the sea. In the tank, those familiar sounds were absent. The only thing he heard were the motors from the filter and pump.

Cleaning the tank was more difficult than he expected. The algae seemed to be glued to the bottom. He had to put all of his body weight into its removal. This task required his full attention - body and mind. He was so involved in this that he didn't notice that he was not alone. As he turned around, the largest dolphin he had ever seen swam towards him. For the first time in his life he felt fearful of an animal.

A huge dolphin face threatened him, with jaws that opened and closed, like two giant pieces of wood slapping together. The dolphin moved his head back and forth, which Orpheus knew was a serious threat. He was trapped against the side of the tank. He knew that there was no way to avoid the wrath of this animal. He stiffened his body and closed his eyes, prepared for the inevitable.

Suddenly he heard a splash. Orpheus opened his eyes and saw Dennis hit the dolphin on his forehead with a long object. The dolphin turned towards his attacker, at which point Dennis grabbed Orpheus by the arm and lifted him out of the pool. Orpheus looked at Dennis with gratitude.

"Why didn't you use one of the pipes at the bottom of the pool? That's what they're there for!" Dennis said.

"No one told me about any pipes, or that I would need them for any reason. I've been swimming with dolphins for years. Never has one tried to hurt me."

"Before you go back into the tank, I think you need to know some basic facts about confined dolphins."

Orpheus nodded.

"After the last show today, come to my cottage, we can have dinner and talk."

Orpheus thanked him again.

*   *   *

Dennis served pan-fried fish. Orpheus took a bite and said, "This tastes great."

"If they are good enough for the dolphin, they are good enough for us."

"You didn't," Orpheus said.

"I did."

Both men laughed. When Orpheus finished his meal he pushed his chair away from the table. "I am stuffed," he said.

"Me too."

"So, what do I need to know about the park, "Orpheus asked, eager to learn as much as possible.

"Jason is not here any more." It is going to be difficult until he can be replaced."

"Why did he leave?"

"Good trainers are hard to find, and harder to keep. Young people such as yourself come here with high ideals and grandiose ideas about working with these animals. Some get disillusioned and leave, others stay and try to make a difference. When they find out that this is a business like any other, some can't cope and move on such as Jason."

Dennis gathered the dishes and put them in the sink. He returned with a bowl of fruit.

"Ivan is not only the largest dolphin in captivity, other than the killer whale, but probably the most aggressive. He weighs nine hundred pounds, and is eleven feet long. Dolphins in captivity act much differently than dolphins in the wild. For instance there is a park that has a dolphin as a companion in the same tank with a killer whale. In the wild the killer whale is a predator. In his natural environment a dolphin might approach and find you interesting for a few minutes but he has the choice to leave at any time. In here that choice isn't available."

"You mean their personalities change in captivity? Are they all dangerous?"

"There's a certain way to handle these animals. Some are less aggressive than others. Like us, they are all different, and have different levels of tolerance." Dennis showed Orpheus the scars on his leg." This is part of the job."

Orpheus recognized the scars, they resembled the raking marks that wild dolphins carried from interaction with each other.

"I didn't hear any clicking noise to alert me that the dolphin was even near." Orpheus said.

"Dolphins don't use echolocation in the tanks because there's nothing to locate, and the acoustics of the concrete tends to reverberate, so the dolphin chooses to turn it off. They are trained to vocalize above the water. In the wild they spend eighty per cent of their time below the surface. When they are brought here eighty per cent of their time is spent above the water. That is why their dorsal fins aren't erect.

"I wondered about that the first time I saw them all together." Orpheus said.

"Dolphins are extremely intelligent animals and will dominate you unless you show them otherwise. Ivan isn't so bad once you get to know him, especially if Penelope is with him. She is much more tolerant of us. Trainers also influence the dolphin's behavior. Some are here because they like to feel superior over the animals, and are abusive in many ways, creating aggression."

Dennis got up and brought a bottle of sherry and two glasses. He poured each of them a glass and began the story about Ivan. "Ivan is the only dolphin in the park who voluntarily jumps the gate to get into the main pool. For some reason dolphins don't jump over things. That is a learned behavior. Just think about where the dolphin lives. They may leap very high out of the water, but there is nothing for them to jump over."

Orpheus had never really thought about that.

"I've heard that a trainer abused Ivan, physically and

emotionally," Dennis said. "Ivan and Penelope were captured together. The trainer loved to torment Ivan by separating the pair. Ivan would vocalize and do everything he knew how to get the trainer to open the gate so that he and Penelope could be together. "One day while the trainer was in the water with Penelope, taunting Ivan, he became so enraged that he leaped over the gate. He grabbed the trainer by his leg and dragged him around the pool, bouncing his body against the side of the tank, until the man was almost dead. Luckily he survived, but no longer works with dolphins. Ivan could have killed him if he wanted to. Since that time, Ivan tests all new trainers. You will have to meet him again to show him who's the boss."

Orpheus sighed, "That may take a little time."

"I can see that you have much to learn."

Orpheus mentally made a vow to himself to be the best and most loving trainer he could be and to never use a weapon against these animals.

Orpheus heard the chimes of the beautiful Grandfather clock in Dennis' cottage and realized how late it was. He stood. "Thank you for dinner. I am grateful for all the help and information."

"Think nothing of it, just stay alert out there. See you tomorrow." Orpheus waved as he said, "Good night!"

The following day when his work was done Orpheus visited the dolphins. Ivan was easy to pick out from the others because of his immense size. The others looked so much alike; it would take time for Orpheus to identify each one. Ivan spotted Orpheus and swam over to him. He did not look as threatening today, but Orpheus was not in the pool. In fact, it seemed that Ivan wanted to play. He retrieved a ball from the other side of the pool and tossed it to Orpheus. Orpheus hurled it to the far end of the tank and Ivan swam to get it. They played this way for some time. He went home that night and felt much better. Thereafter he spent time with Ivan every day, trying to build a trust with him. After a while, Ivan allowed Penelope to join in the games.

One day, Orpheus decided that it was time to confront Ivan in the water. He tossed the ball across the pool. As Ivan went to retrieve it, Orpheus slipped into the water. Ivan dropped the ball from his jaws and sped toward Orpheus. Orpheus planted himself firmly against the side of the tank and looked directly at Ivan. Ivan stopped inches from Orpheus' face and exhibited a threatening posture, jaws snapping. Orpheus remained fixed in his position. After a moment Ivan turned and calmly swam to Penelope, apparently sensing that Orpheus would not harm them. The much anticipated confrontation ended quickly. They were friends.

A few months later it was decided that Penelope was going to another park. No reason was given. Orpheus was very concerned as to how this would affect Ivan. The dolphin who had become Orpheus' friend died five weeks after Penelope's transfer.

The loss of Ivan was very hard on Orpheus. In the months that followed he learned much about how things were done. It was becoming more and more difficult for Orpheus to remain silent. He questioned the decisions made by the "experts" and for the first time thought about leaving the park.

Orpheus and Dennis became good friends. One evening as they were having dinner, Dennis shared the story of Jason and Salty. "Salty was a large, gentle dolphin born at the park. She was easy to work with, the trainers loved her. She never knew what it was like to swim free so she never became aggressive like some of the other dolphins.

"I remember the day Jason was hired. For Salty it was love at first sight. Jason was infinitely patient and spent hours working with her. She would do anything to please him. When she learned a new trick she would claim her fish and a hug from Jason. Or, one of her favorite rewards, she would open her mouth, and Jason would stroke her tongue. When a training session was over and Jason left for the day, Salty would put her beak on the side of the tank and carry on like a child crying for it's mother.

"The public loved to see the dolphins propel their bodies out of the water and appear to walk on their tails. Jason discovered that Salty could do this trick longer than any of the other dolphins. Every day Jason encouraged her to extend her performance. She became known for walking the circumference of the pool by herself. It was the highlight of the dolphin show.

"One day the filter in her pool broke and she needed

to be removed until repairs were completed. She swam onto the stretcher. It took six men to lift her five hundred pound body out of the tank. As Salty was being transferred, one of the men tripped and fell, causing Salty to be dropped. She panicked, her body thrashed wildly. The stretcher wrapped around her tail. Suddenly she stopped moving. She whistled faintly. She was seriously injured.

"When the vet examined Salty he found that several vertebrae in her back had been broken. The only way to save her life was to remove her tail. Salty would never be able to swim again. She could only float and watch the other dolphins perform. When people asked why Salty didn't perform any more they were told that she was older and had been retired.

"Jason did his best to comfort Salty but he could see that she was losing her will to live. She lost weight, despite Jason's efforts to coax her to eat. Eventually, she only accepted food from him.

"Six weeks after the accident, Jason found her lifeless body floating in the pool. He quit the park the same day, without saying good-bye to anyone. That was the day you met him."

"I am beginning to wonder if these dolphins are really as happy as Joseph says they are." Orpheus said. "Maybe they appear to be happy because of their built-in smile."

Dennis nodded in agreement, "I have wondered the same thing myself sometimes."

"Why do you stay?" Orpheus asked.

"Because I don't mistreat them, and I worry that the trainer who replaces me will."

A strong breeze created waves that gently rocked the Seeker. Raindrops fell on Orpheus' face bringing him back to the present time. He had not thought about those days for years. The pain was as vivid now as it had been then.

Hermes

Greek Mytohology

Tricky yet charming character

Hermes

When Orpheus looked up, he saw the Stenella. He hoped that Peter was on board. He dropped the anchor of his small craft into the water, and climbed aboard his friend's vessel. A small seagull sat on the rail, but there was no sign of Peter.

What could have happened to his friend? Did Peter meet some terrible fate? There were no clues. He inspected the Stenella for answers. Nothing. The seagull did not seem frightened, only interested in what was going on. He watched every move Orpheus made. "I'll bet you know what happened to Peter," Orpheus said. "If only you could talk." At that moment, the seagull spread his wings and flew away.

Orpheus felt frustrated. He didn't know whether to look for Peter on the water or stay with the boat and await his return. The bird soared overhead catching various currents of air. His beak pointed toward Orpheus, squawking. "Now what?" Orpheus asked. "Are you hungry?" He threw crumbs of food high into the air. The bird dove and caught each one. Orpheus watched the gull glide close to the water, then finding an updraft, sailed toward the clouds. Orpheus observed the contrast of the pure white bird against the blue sky. His body was perfectly designed for flight with his feet tucked in close to his tail.

As Orpheus' eyes turned from the sky to the water he saw something moving. Through the glare of the sun, fins appeared. A small pod of dolphin. Could this be the dolphins that Peter had told him so much about?

They came straight for the Stenella as if there was a reason for them to be there. They swam alongside and underneath her. They surfaced and dove repeatedly. They scanned the water, as if searching for something. Did they know that Peter was missing?

The sun was setting. Evening turned into nightfall. A breeze was stirring and there was a chill in the air. The brilliance of the full moon acted as an eerie spotlight. The reflection on the water revealed that the dolphins also kept watch. He hoped that by morning he would have a plan. As he lay down to sleep he prayed for help to guide him to his friend.

Orpheus heard the flutter of wings. He looked over to see the little bird perched on the bow of the Seeker. "Where have you been?" Orpheus asked. The gull was unaffected by Orpheus' question as he preened and made himself comfortable. Then he closed his eyes.

"I guess you are staying for the night."

Orpheus left the Stenella anchored where he found it in case Peter returned. He left a note stating his concern and the direction he was going. The journey had barely begun before the seagull was airborne and out of sight.

As Orpheus traveled through familiar waters the dolphins played in the bow wake of the boat. Two at a time would criss-cross in front of the bow, then two more, taking turns, feeling the push from the water. Orpheus marveled at the precision they exhibited swimming in formation with each other while keeping a safe distance from the Seeker. He watched as a calf ventured a little too far from his mother. She whistled to him, but he didn't pay attention. She sped to the young dolphin and disciplined him firmly with her beak. The youngster resumed his place beside her. She didn't return to play in the trail of water, but stayed close to her calf for the next several miles.

Orpheus had traveled North most of the morning. The dolphins were always in sight. He knew they would remain within their home territory, but he would enjoy their company for as long as they decided to stay.

Early in the afternoon the seagull appeared. He flew to his usual place on the bow squawking incessantly. Orpheus threw some crackers his way but the bird was not interested in food. He was visibly distressed. He looked at Orpheus, beak bobbing up and down screeching. Frustrated, Orpheus said, "What is it?" The bird flew away in a westerly direction. "Thank goodness!" Orpheus exclaimed. A few minutes later the seagull returned noisily and flew west again. It appeared that the bird was trying to communicate to Orpheus to change direction and follow him.

Orpheus decided it was worth a try. He guided the boat on her new course and the bird returned seemingly satisfied. Before long the pod of dolphin reappeared. They had ventured well out of their home waters. "I guess we are all in this together," Orpheus said. It wasn't long before the bird took flight again. "I wonder where he goes every day?"

The dolphins remained loyal to the Seeker, never straying far from her side. They found many different things to play with such as kelp, or a feather. A palm frond was good for at least a mile. Later the dolphins found another toy. At first Orpheus couldn't tell what it was. It was pink and looked like a jellyfish. After they grew bored and released it, Orpheus saw that it was a plastic bag which he retrieved from the water. He was glad that they did not try to eat it. He squeezed the excess water from the bag and stuffed it in the container he kept for trash. As evening approached the bird returned as he had the day before.

The next afternoon, the engine on the Seeker started to sputter. Orpheus turned towards shore, hoping to find a town and mechanical help. Within a short time Orpheus spotted a small marina. By now the engine was not working at all and Orpheus had to use the oars to bring the boat to the dock.

Once he secured his small craft, a young man approached, offering assistance. He examined the engine and said that it could be fixed within a few hours. The young man reminded Orpheus of Peter because of his broad smile and his enthusiasm. He had not realized until this moment how empty he felt inside. He decided that while he was waiting he would get something to eat.

He entered the small cafe adjoining the dock, and ordered a hot meal. There were two elderly men in the corner of the room. Their faces looked like leather from spending too many hours in the sun. They both had beards, one neatly trimmed, the other unkempt. Otherwise they could have been twins.

The one closest to Orpheus said, "My name is Tom, this is my brother Tim. What brings you here?"

"I am looking for a young friend of mine. He

is tall and blond. His name is Peter. His experience on the water is limited. We had a severe storm about a week ago, and he has not been seen since. I located his boat but no sign of him."

Both men thought for a moment. "We have not heard of anyone that has been stranded or injured," Tom said.

"The only thing that made recent news," said Tim, "was a couple of fisherman who discovered two dolphins caught in some nets. The authorities removed the mammals and were trying to help them. One looked pretty bad. He had a big ugly scar on his side."

"Do you know where they were taken?" Orpheus asked.

"No, the only thing I know is that several men came with a very large boat and took them."

Orpheus knew by the description of the dolphin that this was Alpha, about whom Peter had talked so much. From his past experiences, Orpheus thought that the two dolphins might have been taken to a captive facility.

At that moment Orpheus realized why the dolphins were following his boat. They were looking for Alpha. He knew that each dolphin played an important role as a member in the community. Despite his knowledge about dolphins in the wild, he was not sure how Alphas' absence would affect the pod.

But where was Peter? Orpheus feared that Peter had met a terrible fate in the storm. Maybe he was hit by lightning. Maybe rough seas had overwhelmed him.

When the Seeker was ready, Orpheus slowly guided her out of the bay and into deeper water where the dolphins were waiting. How could he let them know he was at a dead end and did not know what to do. Should he choose a new direction and continue the search? Maybe he should turn around and go home.

He decided to anchor for the night and see how he felt in the morning. The little seagull had returned and was quietly perched on his favorite spot. Hopefully Orpheus would be guided to make the right decision.

As the sun rose, he sadly decided to return home. The seagull was no where to be seen. The Seeker was underway, with Orpheus thinking about what he would do without Peter. He was filled with sadness.

Suddenly the air was filled with shrieks and squawks. Unexpectedly, the bird returned but something was wrong with him. He perched momentarily on the bow, focused on Orpheus and screamed like a banshee. He flew off only to return and repeat his behavior. Orpheus should have known, the bird realized the Seeker was going in a different direction. He was causing such a commotion, that even the dolphins paid attention. Orpheus wondered if he was trying to guide the Seeker to Alpha and Peter. Was that possible? Something inside of Orpheus encouraged him to follow the seagull. He needed to have faith and go on. He did not know how he would find them, but he knew he had to try.

And so the search would continue, as would the memories that haunted him for the last twenty five years.

Snow

Pure White

Persuade

Charm

Snow

It was mid-summer, many years ago. Orpheus was left at the edge of town with a map, and was warned to stay out of sight. He surveyed the area, found a secluded spot near the water, and proceeded to set up his campsite. He had six weeks to prepare for the capture of the albino dolphin, which the townspeople called Snow.

Orpheus awoke to see the sun barely above the horizon. He lay there, catching glimpses of sky through the branches of a huge live-oak tree. The hanging moss looked like giant spider webs that swayed with the gentle breeze. He thoroughly enjoyed the peacefulness of his surroundings in contrast to the rigid schedule he kept for the past few months at the marine park.

Thoughts of Joseph and the information he shared with Orpheus about the white dolphin were uppermost on his mind. She held a mystical quality for the townspeople. Fishermen boasted that, after seeing the beautiful Snow, they enjoyed unusually large catches. Sometimes she led them to abundant schools of fish.

Once, a young boy fell over the side of a small boat. His frantic parents dove into the water to rescue him. Both came to the surface empty handed. They dove again searching for the child. The second time they reached the surface they heard their son crying. The white dolphin appeared swimming slowly toward the parents, with the child struggling to hold on to her dorsal fin. She came close enough to safely release the child but managed to keep herself just out of reach.

Snow was a protected citizen of the county. Summerville was the only place in the world where it was a felony to remove a dolphin from county waters. Joseph expounded on the selfishness the townspeople showed by their refusal to share the magnificence of Snow. He convinced Orpheus that Snow would benefit from their actions. People would learn about dolphins. Marine experts would care for her and protect her from predators. She would be loved by all, and never have to search for food again. What more could she want? This all sounded logical to Orpheus, even though somewhere inside of him it did not feel right. He shrugged off his doubts.

For the next several days Orpheus strolled along the banks of the water, sometimes walking considerable distances, without any sign of Snow.

Although Joseph had assured Orpheus that Snow always returned, he couldn't help but wonder if this time the capture team had scared her away permanently

A week passed with no sighting. He ventured into town to see what he could find out. A short distance from his campsite he saw children playing. As he approached them he heard one boy say, "I saw her, I'm telling you! She was close to the bridge. I saw her when I crossed it this morning." The excited children ran past Orpheus.

He watched them dart through the palm and oak trees that lined the water. Orpheus attempted to follow them without being noticed. He had been warned by Joseph not to draw any undue attention to himself. The previous capture team had been physically attacked by the concerned citizens, their boat mysteriously destroyed by fire. Joseph felt confident that if the capture could be done at night with the cover of darkness, they had less chance of being discovered.

Although Orpheus kept a safe distance between himself and the children, he heard their excited voices. They approached the bridge. One child screamed, "There she is, I told you!" Orpheus caught sight of a light colored fin. He strained to see her. Just then, she came up to breathe. He saw the top of her body, as she slowly moved towards a sandbar. Small silver fish leaped out of the water trying to escape. She caught one in mid-air swallowing it whole. Then she dove out of sight.

A few minutes later he heard "whoosh." She leaped out of the water. The children screamed with delight. Orpheus was mesmerized by her beauty. She sparkled like a fallen star with the sun reflecting off her wet body. He had never seen anything like her. He watched until she was out of sight. He was so taken by Snow that he failed to realize the children had gone.

He now understood why he had not seen her before. She never passed under the bridge for reasons Orpheus did not understand. He had settled on the wrong side. He hurriedly walked back to his campsite, gathered his belongings and moved them to a new site on the other side of the bridge. He tried to forget the week he had wasted.

The decision to move was a good one. He now saw her on a regular basis. Within a week, Orpheus had a good grasp of Snow's habits. During the day she tended to remain in a secluded area surrounded by mangroves. At night she ventured farther away, possibly to feed. He knew that coastal dolphins fed by day, but this dolphin was not like any other. He swore that she was hiding something behind all that brush.

The day finally came to join her in the water.

She didn't seem to mind as long as he kept his distance and stayed away from her protected area. She looked at him often as if trying to decide whether he was friend or foe. One day Snow approached him. He thought that he could actually feel her sonar scanning his body. He hoped she knew that he meant her no harm.

She was getting used to his presence as he spent progressively more time each day with her in the water. But each time he approached the small inlet, she positioned herself so that Orpheus could not pass. She was gentle but firm in her demands. Orpheus decided to investigate her hiding place at night, when she often disappeared for brief periods. From the surface, Orpheus could not see a visible opening to the inlet. It was covered with overgrowth. He would have to enter from underwater.

The moon was almost full   hopefully providing enough light to discover her secret. Orpheus took his snorkel gear to the water's edge and waited. It was quite late before Snow ventured away.

He slipped into the water to begin his search. As he approached the inlet he made certain that Snow was not around. Days of practice had extended his breathing technique but he still wasn't sure how much time he would need. It was now or never. He surfaced, took a deep breath and swam for the entrance. It turned out to be much easier than he anticipated. A large clearing slightly under water provided easy access.

Once inside, he swam along the narrow body of water, not knowing what he was looking for. What could be so important to the dolphin? As he swam he thought he felt a presence nearby. The moon glimmered on the water but revealed nothing as his eyes searched the surface. He felt a strange sensation pass through his body that he recognized immediately. He saw an unusually small fin pass along- side of him, and heard the familiar "whoosh." It was a calf! Snow was protecting a baby! Could it be hers?

He couldn't tell whether the calf was white or gray. Then he saw a large fin behind the little dolphin. It was definitely white. Snow had returned. She caught him in the act. What would she do? He had always heard that dolphins did not harm humans, but what about a mother protecting her young?

She swam toward him; Orpheus was apprehensive. As she approached the fin appeared larger than he remembered it. Perhaps his fear was affecting his vision. She raced past him to her calf. He felt the power of her tail as it swept within inches of his body. She turned and swam toward Orpheus. When the fin surfaced within a few feet from him, he realized it was not Snow. This dorsal fin was wider and taller, with a slight curve. He realized it was a male.

The dolphin approached Orpheus slowly and deliberately and eyed him with suspicion. Orpheus was not about to stay to find out what this animal was going to do next. He took a deep breath, turned and dove. He swam as fast as he could.

He pulled himself on shore, exhausted, and lay there until he could catch his breath. Questions raced through his mind. Obviously there were a pod of dolphins but were they all albinos? He wondered why the large male had let him get away unhurt. He would have to call and tell Joseph of his discovery.

When he returned to his campsite he built a fire. As the flames dwindled into a flicker Orpheus fell asleep. He dreamed of dolphins that night.

The following morning, thinking more clearly, Orpheus realized that Snow had a family. No one had ever talked about more than one white dolphin. Despite the risk, he had to see the calf in daylight, to determine if it too was an albino. He did not want to create any more stress for the family than was absolutely necessary, but this could mean great things for Orpheus. If they could capture both dolphins and breed them, history would be made. He could see it now. Fame, fortune and living with the animals in harmony. Tomorrow he would call Joseph and tell him of the discovery. Orpheus felt much better about the capture knowing that Snow would be with her family.

For the next two weeks he spent the daylight hours in the water, taking care to stay out of sight of passersby. He entered the inlet whenever anyone approached, giving him more time with the albino family. It saddened him a little to discover that the calf was gray. He hoped that when they were bred in captivity at least one calf would be an albino.

As time went by, Snow and her family began to accept Orpheus. Communication among the dolphins was continual. Identifying whistles followed by a stream of bubbles, squeaks and squawks. They were a noisy group. The calf was the most trusting and adventuresome. He was always ready to play. One of his favorite games involved a piece of kelp. He would offer it to Orpheus. With kelp in hand, Orpheus would swim away as fast as he could and release it. The calf would follow close behind, repossessing the kelp when Orpheus released it. Then he would return the toy, eager to start the game again. Sometimes the adults would play but quickly become bored and go in search of something new.

Snow and the male always stayed close to the calf. Whenever he strayed from their side, either parent would whistle, and the calf returned without hesitation. Orpheus chuckled, observing his obedience, while Snow stroked her offspring lovingly, reinforcing the good behavior.

Orpheus admired the bond that existed among the dolphins. He was also fascinated by the nursing behavior. The calf would nudge Snow's underside, a rich milk was then released, which he quickly consumed. He nursed often, but also ate fish, which led Orpheus to believe he was slightly under one year.

Orpheus discovered that these dolphins spent much of their time playing. They seemed to enjoy just being alive. They playfully sped by Orpheus, buzzing him with their sonar as they passed. Other times they all swam so close that their eyes met. He wondered what they thought. Perhaps because he was able to stay underwater up to four minutes at a time, the dolphins respected him. Orpheus felt a close bond forming, although, only Snow allowed Orpheus to touch her.

He developed an endearing trust with Snow. Soon he was able to guide her through the bridge on a daily basis. Orpheus remembered how visibly afraid Snow was the first time she approached the pillars. As much as she trusted Orpheus, she had an innate fear that intensified whenever they approached the bridge. He wondered what frightened her. Surely her sonar reflected that their was enough open water between the solid pillars for her to pass.

He remembered placing his hands on her body to guide her through. She trembled. But, once past the pillars she was calm and unafraid. It was crucial to move her to the other side of the bridge, into the next county, where the ban on dolphins did not apply.

There were only a few days left for them to share the freedom that Orpheus had come to know and love. He was saddened to know they would not be free, but believed that this small pod would be protected and cared for in their new home. He couldn't bear to imagine something happening to them.

Orpheus received final instructions from Joseph. The capture would occur the following night. Orpheus had to guide Snow into unprotected waters where the first boat would be waiting. As soon as she became visible to the captors, Orpheus would make his exit. After Snow was taken and stabilized they would leave immediately. A second vessel would then enter the inlet and take the male and calf. Orpheus worried about this part of the capture. They would be in protected waters and if caught, consequences would be grave.

The day of the capture was cloudy and dreary. Orpheus prepared to return to the park. He was grateful that he would not to have to watch the capture. He knew it would be stressful for Snow. He had mixed emotions. He deplored the freedom being snatched from his friends, but wanted to help preserve their species for all to appreciate. Orpheus would be glad when it was over and done.

Finally nightfall. Orpheus led Snow away from her family for the last time. As they swam together toward the bridge and beyond, Orpheus strained to see the capture boat. As the lights from the boat got closer Orpheus watched for a signal that Snow had been seen, so he could make his exit. It was important that Snow not make any association between Orpheus and her capture, if they were to work together in the future.

Back at the marine park, Joseph greeted Orpheus with enthusiasm. "You did a magnificent job." He patted Orpheus firmly on the back. "I'm proud of you."

"Thank you sir." Orpheus could not contain his smile.

"You'll find a nice bonus in your next paycheck".

"Oh, thank you," Orpheus said, "Sir, I think it is important that I be the only person to work with Snow and her family. They know and trust me."

"Sure," Joseph said casually, "as long as they are trained and ready to perform soon." With this, Joseph turned and walked toward his office.

*　　　*　　　*

The minutes seemed like hours waiting for Snow's arrival. He waited alongside the pool where they would stay until they were acclimated. His thoughts were of all the wonderful times they were going to have together. No more hiding. Even though he knew they would miss their freedom, he would make it up to them somehow. He would spend all of his time with them. He couldn't wait to share his experiences with the audiences that would come to see her and her family. How proud he would be when they performed the tricks for Orpheus as Ivan had impeccably performed for Hans.

He heard a flurry of activity. They were here! He ran to meet them. The men carefully carried Snow on a stretcher gently spraying water over her body, avoiding the blowhole, to keep her cool. Orpheus entered the pool with Snow as she was being lowered into the water. She did not appear to recognize Orpheus at first. She was sluggish and disoriented. Orpheus thought that it probably was the medication she was given to relieve the stress of the capture and transfer. He held her body and felt her tremble. When he released her she swam slowly around the pool. Orpheus guessed she was trying to determine where she was. Then she swam over to Orpheus and hovered at his side.

Orpheus stayed with Snow for the next few hours, and anxiously waited with her for her family. Once they joined her, he knew she would feel better. He heard men talking loudly. The second capture team was finally here. He left Snow momentarily to observe their arrival.

As he approached he sensed an air of anxiety. He did not see either the calf or the male. Something was terribly wrong. Joseph was there, his face contorted in anger, yelling at the man in charge.

"What do you mean you didn't get them?"

"By the time we found them, someone called the police. We could see them coming. We were lucky to have escaped at all," the man yelled back defensively.

Orpheus was stunned. He couldn't believe what he just heard. He wanted to run and hide, but he knew he had to try to comfort Snow. What would she do now? He was not sure the calf could make it without his mother. There weren't any other female dolphins in that area to help fill the void created by Snow's absence. My God, what had he done?

He was sure the calf would die, and it would be on his conscience for the rest of his life. The tears started to flow as he returned to Snow who would never see her family again. As he entered the pool she seemed to sense his sadness and slowly swam to his side, as if to comfort him.

In the days that followed Snow lost the joyous spirit that Orpheus had come to know so well. She refused to eat. Measures were taken to try to keep her alive, but within three weeks she developed a fatal disease and was gone. She took her last breath in Orpheus' arms.

Orpheus did not know if he could ever forgive himself for the part he had played in Snow's demise, but he did know that he couldn't stay at the park any longer. He packed his things and left a note for Joseph, along with the money that had once been so important to him. He blamed himself for listening to Joseph, when something told him what he was doing was wrong. He felt guilty about taking Snow from her home and her family. Joseph had painted a picture that made sense to Orpheus but living with the dolphins for the past weeks had given him a glimpse into their world. Whatever the drawbacks were for them in the wild they were free. Snow showed him how important that was to her. He should have listened to his heart. He returned to his home, hoping that time would heal his pain.

Peter

Greek origin

Rock or foundation to be built upon.

Peter

The animals needed to be kept calm. Sometimes this was accomplished by talking to them in a soothing manner. Both Peter and Alpha were held in an upright position to keep water away from their blowholes, and prevent them from drowning.

Two women participated in the care of Peter and Alpha. Amy, a twenty-two year old vibrant blonde, and a marine biology student, held Peter. She had volunteered at the Marine Science Center for a brief period of time. She loved caring for the animals in need. But the hard part was letting them go. Harder still was watching the animals die, or witnessing their transfer to marine parks, where unnatural lifestyles caused premature deaths.

An older woman, Helen, tended to Alpha. Helen was more experienced than Amy. And, although she too cared about the animals, her emotions had hardened with time. She stopped crying over the loss of animals years ago. Although she was a large woman whose skin was weathered from extensive exposure to the elements, she was attractive.

Peter heard Alpha whistle faintly. He worried that Alpha might not survive this experience. He tried to communicate to Alpha not to be frightened.

Two men entered the pool and approached Alpha. "We are here for a blood test, to see if this guy's sick," one of them said. He held Alpha while the other man inserted a needle into Alpha's fluke. Then it was Peter's turn. Peter didn't feel any pain, only discomfort, when the needle broke his skin. When the men finished they left.

After a time Alpha was calm. The two women stayed with the dolphins and continued to reassure them. The same men returned again, this time with two others. All four entered the water and approached Alpha. Each had a towel in his hand. They twisted the towels and used them to open Alpha's jaws. One of them forced a long tube down his throat. Clearly afraid, Alpha struggled. Another man poured water from a bottle into the tube, which stretched into Alpha's stomach.

The men turned to Peter. They held him so firmly that he could not have struggled even if he wanted to. They inserted the tube down Peter's throat. He felt a strange sensation as liquid entered his body.

After the men left, Alpha tried to use his echolocation to familiarize himself with the surroundings. But his sonar promptly bounced back without an image. After trying this several times with the same result, he gave up. He communicated to Peter, to try. Peter obtained the same results. Thereafter neither one tried it again.

The men returned periodically to force-feed the dolphins a mixture containing vitamins, antibiotics, and stress medication. They also provided the dolphins with fresh water in this manner.

*   *   *

After a few days Peter began to feel better. Alpha responded as well. They felt more comfortable with the two women. In fact, Peter was becoming quite fond of the younger one. He had heard someone call her Amy. What a lovely name, Peter thought. She was small, her touch was gentle and she had beautiful soft gray eyes. Alpha was getting stronger. The wounds on his skin were healing nicely, and he was starting to look like his old self, except with a few more scars. Amy divided her time between the two captives. Peter hoped that Hermes would not be able to find him. He believed that this was a good time for him to resume his normal image so that he and Alpha could escape. But, every day like clockwork, Hermes came with his daily deposit of seaweed. Peter wondered if he would ever reestablish his life as it was before the storm.

In a short time, Alpha and Peter were strong enough to be left on their own. At first it felt good to be able to swim. But the area was so small that they soon tired of moving in circles and began to look for something else to do. Anything that happened to fall into the tank became a toy. A feather or a piece of paper. Amy brought a ball for them. Alpha enjoyed tossing the ball to anyone who happened to be standing beside the tank, ready or not. He would take the ball on the end of his beak and toss it out of the tank. If anyone picked it up and returned it, Alpha had them. The people tired of the game before he did. To show his anger, he would swim along the side of the pool and as he passed them, slap his powerful tail and create a splash that never failed to get them wet.

One morning Helen and Amy stood alongside the tank talking. Peter and Alpha swam over to where they stood. Peter heard Amy say, "But it is so sad."

Helen put her arm around the young woman and said, "My dear, you need to try not to get so attached to them."

"I know, "tears streamed down Amy's cheeks, "but I can't help it."

"If you're going to become a scientist you'll need to look at them a little differently."

"I know the beautiful dolphin will be accepted, but what about the one with all the scars? The park will have no use for him. What will they do with him?"

"We have informed the officials at the park that they were brought in together. They are going to try to use him for breeding purposes."

Amy looked at Helen, nodding her head, trying to regain her composure.

Peter did not understand what made Amy cry. What was she talking about? Accepting dolphins? Where? For what? What would dolphins do at a park?

Shortly thereafter the men came with a stretcher and lifted Peter and Alpha out of the tank. Each dolphin was deposited into a container lined with soft material, and sprayed with water to keep them cool. Then they were loaded onto a truck.

*   *   *

It was nightfall when they reached their destination. They were placed in another small pool that was identical to the prior enclosure. By now they were hungry. They examined their surroundings carefully. There was nothing to eat.

In fact there was nothing at all, but the two dolphins and water.

The following morning two men came to the pool. Both were young, with athletic bodies. Jeff was tall and thin. He had piercing eyes and a rigid demeanor. The other man, Steve was blond, wore a constant smile and seemed to have a gentleness about him. They stood at the edge of the pool and looked at Alpha and Peter.

"These must be the two that were brought in last night," said Steve. Alpha swam over to examine the two men.

"What are they going to do with the one that has all the scars?" Jeff asked.

"I heard that they are going to put him in the husbandry program."

Jeff looked surprised, "That program hasn't been very successful. Most of the calves born here don't survive, but I guess they want to keep trying."

"Yeah, I guess. I heard that they were caught in some nets."

Steve looked at Alpha with sadness. "Too bad."

Pointing to Peter, Jeff said, "I don't think I've ever seen a more beautiful animal. His skin is flawless. Do they have names?" "I don't think so"

"Why don't we call them Beauty and Beast?

"Steve agreed with an enthusiastic nod.

Steve entered the tank and started to swim.

Alpha eyed him cautiously. After a while Peter and Alpha came close, but nevertheless stayed out of his reach. Jeff, who was still at the edge of the tank, held a bucket. He reached in, pulled out a fish and tossed it to Steve. Alpha and Peter were startled by the sudden movement and sped away. Steve held the fish in his hand. Peter stared at it. Steve said, "Come on Beauty, taste it. You too, Beast. You have to eat something." This went on for some time but the dolphins refused to eat.

Jeff entered the pool while Steve stayed at the edge. Alpha sped past Jeff and slapped his tail, almost hitting him in the face. Peter could not believe it but Alpha was aggressively taunting Jeff. Every time Jeff entered the pool Alpha repeated his aggressive behavior. There was something about Jeff that Alpha did not like.

Jeff said, "I have had enough. From now on you get in the water and I'll stay here and observe."

Steve agreed. He slipped into the water cautiously. Alpha looked at him but made no move toward him.

Steve held a fish out for the dolphins. Alpha sped over to examine it, without getting too close. The fish was dead, therefore it had no appeal. Alpha refused to eat it even though he was hungry. Alpha continued to swim around the tank. A few minutes later Alpha swam over to Steve and seized the fish out of Steve's hand. He playfully tossed it to Peter. A new toy! Peter couldn't understand why the man kept placing dead fish in the water.

By the third day, the pair was ravenous and sluggish from lack of nourishment. Steve, along with two other men, force-fed them again. Steve suggested that they introduce Beauty and Beast to a resident dolphin already trained to eat dead fish.

Lucky was an even-tempered female bottlenose that had done well in captivity. She had learned quickly what was expected of her and seldom gave anyone trouble. She was soft gray and relatively small. She had a scar on her lower jaw from a rambunctious male who greeted her roughly when she first arrived at the park. She was about ten years old and had reached maturity. She would deliver her first calf in a few months.

She had beached herself along with an adult male and female, probably her mother and father, about eight years ago. She was the lone survivor, that is how she came to be called Lucky. As the gate opened and Lucky entered, both Alpha and Peter watched her cautiously. As she came through the gate she saw the fish all over the bottom of the tank, she swam from one to the other and consumed them as if she had not eaten in a week. After devouring all of them, she came over and examined the new additions.

Alpha's response was less than friendly. Although Alpha communicated with Lucky, Peter knew from Alpha's body language that he was frustrated and angry with the confinement. Lucky communicated that if they were hungry, they should eat what was being offered.

The next day the fish was again offered and this time Peter tried one. It wasn't the same as live prey but it satisfied his hunger. Following Peter's lead, Alpha also ate. Together they devoured an entire bucket of fish. In the afternoon, the trainers brought another bucket-full. Steve held his arm high in the air with a fish in his hand. Alpha jumped out of the water and took it from him. Peter liked this idea. They were eating and having fun at the same time.

As the days progressed Peter did well at the park, learning new behaviors, jumping over poles, and taking fish out of the trainer's mouths. Alpha was another story. He became bored easily and continued exhibiting his frustration, regardless of Peter's attempts to reassure him. Whenever Steve finished feeding them, Alpha would deliberately bump him so as to knock him over in the shallow water. Then he would swim in circles to create a whirlpool effect and keep Steve off- balance.

The trainers challenged Peter to jump higher and higher. Peter was always hungry and quickly learned to do whatever was required to get fed.

Alpha also learned that a trick earned him a fish. Each time they performed a trick they went to a designated area which was called a feeding station to collect a reward.

The dolphins also learned to clean their own tanks. Any kind of debris that was brought to the trainer was rewarded with a fish. Alpha was particularly good at this. One day he brought a piece of paper to Steve and received his usual reward. Then he brought another piece of paper. Steve noticed that the paper looked very much the same. After several rewards were given, Steve discovered that Alpha had torn a paper bag into small pieces in order to get more fish.

Steve marveled at the intelligence of the dolphins. Many times he wondered who was the trainer and who was the trainee. He spent most of his time testing the dolphins' limits. They had an awareness of themselves that most animals did not have.

Alpha's behavior became more aggressive. Jeff had refused to enter the tank with him some time ago, but now Steve was also apprehensive, especially after the hula-hoop incident. The trainers had been trying to get the dolphins to leap through the hoop in mid-air. To start to learn the trick a hula-hoop was placed in the water and the trainer held a fish on the other side. As soon as the dolphin passed through the hoop he would receive his reward.

Alpha had refused to do this trick. He went around, over and under, but refused to pass through. Steve would not give him the fish until Alpha did what was asked. Two days had passed, and Alpha was starving. He finally attacked Steve out of desperation. He deliberately rammed into him with the side of his body. Steve was taken to the hospital with two cracked ribs. Thereafter Steve refused to work with him at all.

Peter heard the trainers talking about alternatives for Alpha. "We could put him in an isolation tank. Maybe a couple of days with no food, no human contact, and a space that he can't turn around in might teach him a lesson about just how good he has it here. "Jeff said.

"I think that will only make it worse." Steve said.

"We can't transfer him to another park because he's so mean. And even if he wasn't, he couldn't work a show the way he looks, with all those scars. What do you suggest?"

"I think that Beast has been through a lot. Maybe he's just afraid to trust anyone. He's very good with Beauty."

"Beauty is the only one that he's good with. He won't mate with a female, which is why he was brought here in the first place. When we decided to call him Beast I guess we didn't know how right we were."

The owner of the park decided that the only alternative was to set him free. Because he had been in captivity a few short weeks, it was believed he would be able to take care of himself. Peter heard this. Although he was glad that Alpha would be released, he feared Alpha would not survive alone so far from his home territory. Peter thought that his fate also was sealed as long as Hermes continued to bring the seaweed. He felt helpless.

It was evening. Alpha and Peter had their usual race around the pool. Jeff and Steve appeared with two other men who carried a large net and a stretcher. Peter knew what was about to happen. He was angry and, for the first time, was not about to hide it. When Steve entered the water Peter swam directly toward him intending to attack. The next thing he felt was a blow to his head. He felt pain and swam to the other side of the tank where he remained until they had Alpha in the net and under control. He sadly watched his friend being taken away.

After Alpha was gone, Peter wondered if his fate was to remain in dolphin form forever. As he swam around the tank feeling sadness for himself and for Alpha, he grew tired, finding it difficult to swim. What Peter didn't realize until this moment was that Hermes had not come today. He looked down into the tank and saw he had feet instead of flukes, and his fins were now becoming hands. As the process continued he looked around to make sure no one had seen what was happening.

At last he was no longer Beauty but Peter. He pulled himself out of the pool and frantically looked for something to cover his naked body. He did not want to get caught, with or without clothes.

He found his way to the area where the trainers changed their clothes. He prayed that he would find something in the darkness. He reached for what felt like a pair of shorts and put them on. They were a little small but they would do. He searched for a mirror to see how he looked.

As he exited the dressing area, he saw Steve approach. Peter panicked for an instant and then struggled to compose himself. As Steve came closer, Peter looked directly into his eyes and extended his hand.

"Hi, my name is Peter, I'm new here. I'm in a hurry so I'll catch you later," Peter shook Steve's hand and briskly walked away.

"Nice to meet you Peter," Steve said to Peter's back. Steve had the strangest feeling that they had met before.

Orpheus had traveled far. He was exhausted, but felt that he was close to finding some answers about Peter. He heard that two dolphins had been brought here after they were found near the Stenella. One of them sounded like Alpha, the dolphin Peter had talked so much about. Maybe the men who found them had some information about Peter.

Orpheus entered the park. He knocked on the office door. The man behind the door asked, "What do you want?"

"I understand that you have two newly acquired dolphins that were captured far from here. Can you tell me anything about them? I am searching for a young man that might have been with them at the time of their capture."

The man became agitated. "We had two dolphins here a few days ago. I don't know anything about anyone being with them when they were found. "One was uglier than sin and had a mean streak. We had to let him go yesterday. He came in with another dolphin that has mysteriously disappeared."

"How does a dolphin disappear?"

"All I know is that one of my trainers went to check on the dolphin last night and ran into someone named Peter who said he worked here. We don't have anyone employed here by that name. This morning the dolphin was gone. I think he must have stolen the dolphin somehow."

"Could you tell me what this man named Peter looked like?"

"The trainer who saw him said he was young, tall, kind of skinny, blonde hair. That's all I know."

Orpheus thought, at last he had found Peter. He was safe! He was sure that Peter must be close. He left the park with renewed vigor. He went to the nearest marina and asked if anyone fitting Peter's description had been there in the last few days. No one had seen him. Orpheus spent the whole day asking people about Peter. But it was as if he dropped off the face of the earth.

Something very strange was going on. Orpheus felt angry and frustrated. He had come so far, gotten so close, but still had not found his friend.

As he walked back to the Seeker, he attempted to sort things out. The man at the park had described Peter. But, why hadn't anyone else seen him? Could he have freed the captive dolphin? And if so, how did he do it? As all of these thoughts were in Orpheus' mind, he found comfort in sensing that Peter was alive. Maybe Peter didn't want Orpheus to find him, although something deep inside told him that someday they would be reunited.

Orpheus felt that he was at a dead end. That night he made the painful decision to return home. The next morning Orpheus prepared for the long journey. He wondered what the future held for Alpha and Peter, as well as for himself. The trip back would give him time to make plans for his own future. As the Seeker began to move in the water, Hermes took flight.

Peter fell asleep at the water's edge, hoping to see some sign of Alpha. As he awoke he scanned the water, but no sign of his friend. He decided to take a swim before determining what to do next. He enjoyed the feeling of the salt water on his body, it felt wonderful.

He took a deep breath and swam under the surface, enjoying all the things that he had missed. The sounds of the sea and the beauty of live plants moving gracefully in the water. Fish swimming in pursuit of prey. Above all, he was free.

He swam for an hour before needing to rest. He floated on his back, looking up at the clouds in the sky and remembering all the times with Alpha, good and bad. Suddenly something bumped him from under the water, startling him. As he rolled over on to his stomach and began to swim it bumped him again. He dove under the water to get a better look. He heard the clicking. When he surfaced he heard the familiar whoosh. Sure enough, it was Alpha! In the excitement he swallowed mouthfuls of salt water. Peter was elated to see his friend.

They joyfully swam together with Peter holding Alpha's fin." We just have to figure out how to get home now," said Peter. Just then, they heard the squawking of Hermes overhead with his beak full of seaweed. Now they would find their way home together...

Glossary

Alpha:
Greek origin: First or   beginnings

Aphrodite:
Greek Mythology: Goddess of love

Apollo:
Greek Mythology: Sun God
Optimism ~ abundant energy

Aristotle:
Greek philosopher: Natural scientist in
the fourth century B.C. He was the first to classify
dolphins as mammals.

Hermes:
Greek Mythology: Tricky yet charming character
renouned for his mischievous pranks. He was a
messenger who communicated between earth and
heavens, between Gods and men.

Orpheus:
Greek Mythology: Qualities of dynamism and
creativity through water. Element as a wish to form
personal relationships and help other people.

Peter:
Greek origin: Rock or foundation to be built upon.

Book			Qty	$ AMT
1-12	@	$11.95 *each*	_____	_____
12 - 24	@	$10.75 *each*	_____	_____
24 or more	@	$ 9.50 *each*	_____	_____

Merchandise Total $_____

Florida Tax 6% $_____
Shipping
2.00 first item $_____
.75 each additional item $_____

TOTAL $ [_____]

Please Ship To

Name_____

Address_____

_____

City_____St.____ Zip_____

Please send check payable to:
Dolphin Defenders
P.O. Box 933
Bonita Springs, FL 34133
Phone: 941 947-2268 Fax 941 498-2879

Please allow 4-6 weeks for delivery